AL-QAE

The upcoming Attack on the United States
and Europe Unveiled

AL-QAEDA 2.0

The Upcoming Attack on the United States and Europe Unveiled

William Archer

For the
Transatlantic Intelligence Consortium

Author: The Transatlantic Intelligence Consortium
Coverdesign: The Transatlantic Intelligence Consortium
ISBN: 9798338313640

"What America and its allies fear the most is that we take the battlefield from Kabul, Baghdad and Gaza to Washington, London, Paris and Tel Aviv and to take it to all the American, Jewish and Western interests in the World"

Hamza Bin Laden
Emir Al-Qaeda

About the Author and contributors

The information in this book from the Transatlantic Intelligence Consortium comes from a small group of former intelligence officers and agents from the US and Europe, brought together by a common purpose and a shared history. Our journey into the world of intelligence began in the wake of the tragic events of September 11, 2001 - a day that not only changed the world but also profoundly shaped our professional lives. The devastation wrought by Al-Qaeda on that fateful day fueled our commitment to safeguarding our nations from the threats posed by global terrorism. Since then, our lives have been dedicated to understanding, infiltrating, and combating this resilient and dangerous organization.

We have spent decades at the forefront of the fight against Al-Qaeda. Our work has taken us across the globe, from the bustling streets of Western capitals to the remote, unforgiving terrains of the Middle East and South Asia. We have engaged in complex counterterrorism operations, built intricate networks of human resources and gathered intelligence that has been critical in preventing numerous attacks. Through our respective roles, we have developed a deep and nuanced understanding of Al-Qaeda's inner workings, leadership dynamics, and evolving tactics.

Our collective expertise is beyond theoretical; it is grounded in real-world experience and firsthand encounters with some of the most dangerous individuals on the planet. We have worked tirelessly to infiltrate Al-Qaeda's ranks, and gained insights that have proven invaluable to global counterterrorism efforts. Our backgrounds in human intelligence (HUMINT) have taught us the importance of building trust with our sources - often under incredibly challenging and life-threatening circumstances.

Following the fall of Kabul in August 2021, we recognized an urgent need to adapt and expand our intelligence-gathering efforts. All the Western Afghan sources had their phones shut off on August 30th 2021, something that had felt like a 'digital guillotine' to them, they knew they were abandoned. The rapid changes in Afghanistan's political landscape, coupled with the resurgence of the Taliban, created a volatile environment that Al-Qaeda could exploit to regroup and plan new attacks.

Over the past three years, we have successfully built a vast and reliable intelligence network that now includes over 50 sources, many of whom are embedded close to the Taliban and Al-Qaeda leadership.

This network has provided us with unparalleled access to information that is both credible and detailed. By adhering to the principle of "one source = no source," we have meticulously cross verified every piece of intelligence, ensuring its accuracy before drawing any conclusions. This rigorous approach has allowed us to compile a comprehensive picture of Al-Qaeda's current activities, strategies, and, most alarmingly, its plans for future attacks.

The intelligence gathered points to a chilling and imminent threat intended to surpass the horrors of 9/11. This threat compels us to write this book and share our findings. We hope that our insights will help raise awareness, encourage preparedness, and ultimately contribute to a safer world.

The fight against terrorism is far from over, more than ever, it requires the vigilance and cooperation of all who value peace and security.

Table of Contents

Introduction

Overview of the threat

In the aftermath of the devastating attacks on September 11, 2001, the world witnessed the immense capability of Al-Qaeda to execute large-scale terrorist operations with catastrophic results. That fateful day changed the global security landscape forever and lead to significant advancements in counterterrorism efforts and intelligence gathering. Despite these measures, Al-Qaeda remains a persistent and evolving threat.

Today, new intelligence has emerged from reliable sources close to Al-Qaeda's leadership and from Human Intelligence (HUMINT) operations on the ground in Afghanistan. This intelligence reveals a chilling plan - one that aims to launch a series of coordinated attacks across the United States and Europe that would eclipse the horrors of 9/11. If carried out, these attacks will result in unprecedented loss of life, economic devastation, and psychological trauma.

This book seeks to inform and prepare readers by shedding light on the gravity of this emerging threat. By making this information public, we aim to warn citizens and encourage proactive measures to mitigate the potential impact of this attack.

Background on Al-Qaeda

To understand the current threat posed by Al-Qaeda, it is essential to revisit the history of this organization and its evolution over the past few decades. Founded in the late 1988 by Osama Bin Laden, Al-Qaeda quickly rose to prominence as a global jihadist network committed to attacking Western targets and overthrowing governments in the Muslim world it deemed apostate. The organization's ideology is rooted in a radical interpretation of Islam, advocating for violent jihad against those it considers enemies of Islam.

The attacks on September 11, 2001 culminated years of planning and marked Al-Qaeda's most significant strike against the United States. The terrorist attack killed nearly 3.000 people and the world watched in horror as the twin towers of the World Trade Center collapsed. This event spurred a global "War on Terror," leading to the dismantling of Al-Qaeda's bases in Afghanistan and the death of its leader, Osama Bin Laden, in 2011.

However, despite these setbacks, Al-Qaeda proves-to be resilient. Under the leadership of Ayman al-Zawahiri and his successors, Saif Al-Adl, and the 'Bin Laden brothers', the organization adapted, decentralized its operations, and continued to inspire and direct attacks worldwide. Over the years, it forged alliances with other jihadist groups, extended its reach through various regional affiliates, and refined its strategies to adapt to the changing global landscape. Today, Al-Qaeda is the biggest threat to global security - driven by a renewed focus on large-scale attacks to cause maximum casualties and sow fear.

The primary aim of this book is to warn. The information presented here is to prepare and inform. In an era where terrorism has become a complex and ever-evolving threat, public awareness and vigilance are crucial components of national security. Understanding the nature of the threat we face is the first step in preventing it.

By bringing to light the details of Al-Qaeda's latest plot, we hope to spur action at both governmental and community levels. This book delves into the specifics of the uncovered plan, provide insights into Al-Qaeda's current operational tactics, activities and capabilities, and discuss the potential impacts of the proposed attacks. Additionally, we explore practical measures individuals, communities, and governments can take to enhance their preparedness and resilience in the face of such threats.

The information in this book is based on credible HUMINT intelligence gathered from Afghanistan and other key regions. Our sources, deeply embedded within Al-Qaeda's network, risked their lives to ensure this intelligence reaches us, and thus the public. It is now our collective responsibility to heed these warnings and take the necessary steps to protect ourselves, our loved ones, and our nations from impending danger.

As you read this book, we encourage you to stay informed, remain vigilant, and spread awareness within your communities. Terrorism thrives on fear and ignorance, but with knowledge, preparation, and unity, we can thwart nefarious plans and safeguard our future.

We cannot stop this attack; the plan is set in motion. Al-Qaeda, in the past three years, trained and executed the first parts of the plot and its fighters, the ones executing the plan, are already amongst us. They arrived in the past years with the large streams of immigrants to Europe and to the US.

The threat we face is more than a matter for governments or security agencies; it is a challenge for every one of us. The ability of Al-Qaeda to execute a plot of this magnitude hinges on our collective complacency and underestimation of their capabilities. Understanding the enemy is the first step in defeating them. By being informed and prepared, we can deny these terrorists the success they seek and protect the values we hold dear.

This book is a call to action. It is a reminder that freedom and safety are never guaranteed - they are preserved through vigilance, resilience, and the unyielding commitment to protect one another. We must act now to ensure that the horrors of the past are never repeated and that our future remains secure from those who seek to destroy it.

With this knowledge, let us not wait for the storm to strike. Instead, let us be the force that rises to defend our communities, and our way of life. The time to act is now.

The Post 9/11 Evolution

A New Era of Terrorism

The catastrophic events of September 11, 2001 represented a watershed moment in the history of terrorism, reshaped the global security landscape, and altered the way the world perceives and responds to terrorist threats. The attacks, orchestrated by Al-Qaeda, demonstrated an unprecedented level of coordination, scale, and audacity, which forever changed the nature of international terrorism. Al-Qaeda's ability to strike at the heart of the United States with such devastating impact revealed not only the vulnerabilities of modern societies but also the evolving capabilities of terrorist organizations.

Before 9/11, terrorist attacks were often seen as localized or region-specific, typically associated with political or ideological conflicts within specific countries. The 9/11 attacks illustrated that terrorism had transcended these boundaries, a global phenomenon with the capability to target powerful nations far from the immediate conflict zones. The sheer scale of the attacks, which resulted in the deaths of nearly 3,000 people and caused unprecedented damage, underscored the need for a reevaluation of counterterrorism strategies worldwide.

The response to the attacks established a global counterterrorism framework characterized by significant changes in policy, intelligence-sharing, and security practices. The U.S. government, along with its allies, initiated the War on Terror, which involved military interventions in Afghanistan and Iraq, aimed at dismantling terrorist networks and removing hostile regimes that supported them. This period saw the creation of new agencies, such as the Department of Homeland Security (DHS) and the National Counterterrorism Center (NCTC), as well as significant reforms in intelligence and law enforcement practices.

The Transformation of Terrorist Tactics and Strategies

The years following 9/11 witnessed a notable shift in the tactics and strategies employed by terrorist organizations. Al-Qaeda, once renowned for its centralized, large-scale operations, began to adapt its approach in response to increased pressure from global counterterrorism efforts. This adaptation was driven by the need to evade detection and maintain operational effectiveness despite the intense scrutiny and disruption faced by the organization.

One significant change was Al-Qaeda's move towards decentralization. In the early 2000s, the organization's leadership, under the direction of Osama Bin Laden and his deputy Ayman al-Zawahiri, recognized the risks associated with maintaining a highly visible, centralized structure. The relentless pursuit of Al-Qaeda's leaders by U.S. and allied forces, culminating in the death of Bin Laden in 2011, further accelerated this shift. Al-Qaeda's strategy evolved to emphasize a more dispersed and autonomous network of affiliates and cells, each operating independently but united by a shared ideology and strategic goals.

This decentralization led to a rise in the prominence of local and regional terrorist groups who pledged allegiance to Al-Qaeda or were inspired by its ideology. Groups like Al-Qaeda in the Arabian Peninsula (AQAP), Al-Qaeda in the Islamic Maghreb (AQIM), and Al-Shabaab in Somalia became prominent players in the global jihadist movement. These affiliates, while maintaining their local operational focus, also coordinated with the central leadership, contributed to a broader and more complex global network of terrorism.

The shift towards decentralized operations also gave rise to the phenomenon of lone-wolf attacks and small-cell operations. The increased use of these tactics made it more challenging for intelligence agencies to detect and prevent terrorist activities. Rather than orchestrating grand, coordinated attacks, Al-Qaeda and its affiliates inspired and incited individuals to carry out smaller, less predictable acts of terrorism. This approach was exemplified by attacks such as the 2013 Boston Marathon bombing, carried out by the Tsarnaev brothers, who were motivated by extremist ideologies propagated online.

The Rise of New Terrorist Entities and the Spread of Global Jihad

In the years following 9/11, the global jihadist movement saw the emergence of new terrorist entities that both complemented and competed with Al-Qaeda. One of the most significant developments was the rise of the Islamic State of Iraq and Syria (ISIS), also known as Daesh. Originally an offshoot of Al-Qaeda in Iraq (AQI), ISIS was founded by Abu Musab al-Zarqawi, who led AQI's efforts to establish an Islamic state in Iraq. Following Zarqawi's death in 2006, the group underwent several transformations before rebranding itself as ISIS under the leadership of Abu Bakr al-Baghdadi.

In 2014, ISIS declared the establishment of a caliphate, capturing large swathes of territory in Iraq and Syria. This declaration marked a significant departure from Al-Qaeda's approach, focusing on territorial control and governance rather than purely terrorist operations. ISIS's ability to govern, enforce its interpretation of Islamic law, and attract foreign fighters from around the world represented a new chapter in the evolution of jihadist groups. The group's sophisticated use of social media and online propaganda allowed it to recruit followers, spread its ideology, and inspire attacks globally.

The rise of ISIS led to a complex dynamic within the global jihadist movement. Al-Qaeda and ISIS were ideologically similar but had different strategies and goals. This division fractured the jihadist movement with some groups aligning with ISIS while others remained loyal to Al-Qaeda. Violent confrontations marked the competition between these groups such as the clashes between ISIS and Al-Qaeda affiliates in Syria. Despite this fragmentation, both Al-Qaeda and ISIS continue to influence and inspire terrorist activities worldwide.

The spread of global jihadist ideology also facilitated the rise of lone actors and small cells inspired by extremist propaganda. Individuals radicalized online or through extremist literature carried out attacks independently, without direct affiliation with established terrorist groups. This trend evidenced in high-profile attacks such as the 2015 Paris attacks carried out by the Bataclan and Stade de France attackers, and the 2016 Brussels bombings, orchestrated by individuals inspired by ISIS's messaging.

Continued Threats and the Resurgence of Al-Qaeda

While ISIS dominated global headlines in the mid-2010s, Al-Qaeda remained a persistent and evolving threat. The group's resilience and adaptability allowed it to survive and even thrive despite the intense pressure from counterterrorism efforts. Al-Qaeda's strategy during this period focused on rebuilding its networks, strengthening its regional affiliates, and maintaining a long-term vision for jihadist goals.

Under the leadership of Ayman al-Zawahiri, who succeeded Osama Bin Laden, Al-Qaeda continued to emphasize the importance of patience and persistence in the struggle against the West and its allies. Al-Zawahiri, who had been a key figure in Al-Qaeda's ideological development and operational planning, maintained a focus on the organization's traditional goals, including the overthrow of "apostate" regimes in the Muslim world and the establishment of an Islamic caliphate through a more gradual process.

Al-Qaeda's affiliates played a crucial role in the group's resurgence. Al-Qaeda in the Arabian Peninsula (AQAP), led by figures like Nasir al-Wuhayshi, and later Qasim al-Raymi, became known for its operational capabilities and involvement in high-profile attacks, such as the Charlie Hebdo shooting in Paris. Al-Qaeda in the Islamic Maghreb (AQIM), under the leadership of Abdelmalek Droukdel, expanded its influence in North Africa and the Sahel region. Al-Shabaab, led by Ahmed Abdi Godane, continued its insurgency in Somalia, aligning with Al-Qaeda's global jihadist agenda.

The reemergence of Al-Qaeda as a significant player in global terrorism was further facilitated by the chaotic geopolitical landscape in the Middle East and North Africa. The Syrian Civil War, for example, created an environment in which various jihadist groups, including Al-Qaeda affiliates, could operate with relative impunity. The conflict also provided opportunities for these groups to recruit, train, and launch attacks within the region and beyond.

The Shift in Focus: Afghanistan and Beyond

The Taliban's takeover of Afghanistan in August 2021 marked a critical juncture for Al-Qaeda and its operations. The fall of Kabul represented a significant strategic development for the group, as Afghanistan, once again, became a safe haven for Al-Qaeda's leadership and operatives. The Taliban's return to power provided Al-Qaeda with new opportunities to regroup, train, and plan without the immediate threat of being targeted by international forces.

The relationship between the Taliban and Al-Qaeda is complex and multifaceted. The two groups share ideological affinities and have a history of cooperation dating back to the pre-9/11 era when the Taliban provided sanctuary to Al-Qaeda operatives. However, the Taliban's need for international legitimacy, and its desire to avoid further conflict with Western powers, necessitate a careful balancing act. Al-Qaeda must navigate this relationship to avoid actions that might jeopardize the Taliban's position or provoke international intervention.

The strategic implications of the Taliban's takeover extend beyond Afghanistan's borders. The resurgence of the Taliban and the strengthening of Al-Qaeda's position in Afghanistan raise concerns about the broader regional and global security environment. The increased collaboration between Al-Qaeda and other jihadist groups, both in Afghanistan and elsewhere, will have far-reaching consequences for international counterterrorism efforts.

As we examine the evolution of terrorism since 9/11, it is clear the landscape is characterized by constant change and adaptation. Terrorist organizations like Al-Qaeda have demonstrated an ability to evolve their tactics, strategies, and alliances in response to shifting circumstances. This adaptability makes them a persistent and formidable threat, necessitating ongoing vigilance and innovation in counterterrorism strategies.

The evolution of terrorism in the post-9/11 era has also highlighted the need for a comprehensive and nuanced understanding of the threats we face. As terrorist organizations continue to adapt and evolve, so too must our approaches to addressing and mitigating these threats.

By examining the transformations in terrorism over the past two decades, we can better anticipate and respond to the challenges that lie ahead.

The Bond Between Al-Qaeda and the Taliban

To fully understand the dynamics of Al-Qaeda's current position and its evolving strategies, it's crucial to examine the intricate relationship between Al-Qaeda and the Taliban. Although this relationship has been significant since before 9/11, it has grown even more crucial in recent years. The bond between these two entities is anchored in a pledge of allegiance known as the bay'ah—a term from Arabic that signifies a solemn oath of loyalty. This pledge was first made in the 1990s when Osama Bin Laden swore allegiance to Mullah Omar, the then-leader of the Taliban. Since then, this pledge has been renewed and reaffirmed multiple times, underscoring the deep connection between the two groups.

In the Islamic context, the bay'ah represents a formal promise of loyalty to a Muslim leader and is foundational for loyalty among jihadist groups. It imposes obligations on both parties, including the adherence of the one making the bay'ah to the leader's commands. Violating this pledge is considered a serious offense in Islam and can have severe repercussions.

For Al-Qaeda, the bay'ah means the group has effectively subordinated itself to the Taliban. By making this pledge, Al-Qaeda members acknowledge the Taliban leader and his successors as their superiors, who carry the title Amir al-Mu'minin or Commander of the Faithful. The current leader of the Taliban, Hibatullah Akhundzada, holds this title. He is regarded as the 'supreme leader' within the Taliban, while Sirajuddin Haqqani, a prominent Taliban figure, holds the title of Caliph or Khalifah.

These titles have nuanced meanings within the context of the Taliban. The Kandahari Taliban, under Akhundzada's leadership, focus on their local emirate and view him as the Amir al-Mu'minin. On the other hand, the Haqqani Network regards its leader as the leader of all Muslims globally, which explains why he carries the title Khalifah. These distinctions reflect differing visions and goals within the Taliban itself.

The pledge of allegiance from Al-Qaeda to the Taliban was a crucial factor in Mullah Omar's refusal to hand over Osama Bin Laden to the United States after the 9/11 attacks. Surrendering Bin Laden would have been a grave breach of the bay'ah.

A notable example of what can occur when the bay'ah is disregarded was seen in Al-Qaeda's branch in Iraq, led at the time by Abu Musab al-Zarqawi. Zarqawi's refusal to adhere to his pledge of loyalty to Al-Qaeda's central command was met with severe criticism from Bin Laden, particularly over Zarqawi's violent attacks on Shia Muslims, which Bin Laden deemed excessive. The tension escalated to the point where Bin Laden threatened to expel Zarqawi from Al-Qaeda. This conflict ultimately led to a split: Al-Qaeda in Iraq disassociated itself and evolved into what is now known as the Islamic State (ISIS).

Following the death of Osama Bin Laden in 2011, Ayman al-Zawahiri, who succeeded Bin Laden as Al-Qaeda's leader, renewed the pledge of allegiance to Mullah Omar to reaffirm the close ties between Al-Qaeda and the Taliban.

In 2014, after ISIS declared its caliphate in parts of Iraq and Syria, this pledge was reaffirmed once more. Al-Zawahiri's renewed pledge of allegiance was published in Al-Qaeda's newsletter, issued by their media arm, As-Sahab. Interestingly, later in my career, I became involved with the work of this media branch.

After Mullah Omar's death, Ayman al-Zawahiri renewed his pledge to the new Taliban leader, Mullah Akhtar Mohammad Mansour, in August 2015. In this pledge, he committed to "the jihad to liberate every inch of occupied Muslim land." Mansour acknowledged this pledge and viewed it as a clear endorsement of Al-Qaeda's global jihadist agenda, which contrasted sharply with the Taliban's more localized focus on implementing Islamic governance within Afghanistan and maintaining normal relations with neighboring countries.

When Haibatullah Akhundzada assumed leadership of the Taliban following Mansour's death (killed in a U.S. airstrike in May 2016), Al-Zawahiri's pledge of allegiance was not publicly recognized by the Taliban. This lack of public acknowledgment, combined with the fact that the pledge was not repudiated, has led to some confusion and uncertainty in the West regarding the current status of the relationship between Al-Qaeda and the Taliban.
However, within Al-Qaeda and the Taliban, there is no doubt about the close bond they share.

Today, the two groups are virtually intertwined through a renewed pledge of allegiance made by Al-Zawahiri's successors (the Bin Laden Brothers) in Kandahar in 2022 and also through intermarriages. Hamza Bin Laden is married to a daughter of Taliban Founder Mullah Omar, their son is Named 'Osama Bin Laden' and his grandfathers are Osama Bin Laden and Mullah Omar. The presence of Al-Qaeda members in key positions within the Taliban administration underlines the close ties. These close ties grant the Taliban significant credibility within hardline jihadist circles. The historical loyalty of the Taliban to Al-Qaeda means they are unlikely to abandon their influential ally now that they are in power.

This relationship demonstrates the bond between Al-Qaeda and the Taliban is deeply rooted in mutual ideological alignment, shared history, and common interests. The pledge of allegiance, or bay'ah, remains the cornerstone of their alliance and continues to play a crucial role in shaping their joint actions and strategies.

Understanding Global Jihad

The concept of global jihad is often misunderstood in the context of contemporary terrorism. To grasp the motivations and objectives of jihadist groups such as Al-Qaeda and ISIS, it is essential to delve into the theological and historical underpinnings of jihad in Islam. One must explore the religious foundations of global jihad, the ideological evolution of jihadist movements, and the implications of their quest for a global Islamic state.

The Theological Foundations of Jihad

In Islam, jihad originally meant "struggle" or "striving" and encompassed both personal and collective dimensions. It is derived from the Arabic root jhd, which signifies exertion or effort. The concept is multidimensional, including spiritual, moral, and physical struggles. The spiritual struggle involves striving to live a righteous life according to Islamic principles, while the physical struggle can encompass defense against oppression or aggression.

Quranic Injunctions and Hadith

The Quran and Hadith provide the primary sources for understanding jihad. The Quran, Islam's holy book, includes several verses that address the concept of jihad. For example, Surah Al Baqarah (2:190) states, "Fight in the way of Allah those who fight you but do not transgress the limits. Indeed, Allah does not like transgressors." This verse outlines the ethical parameters of jihad, emphasizing fighting is only permitted in self-defense and should not exceed the bounds set by Islamic law.

The Hadith, the recorded sayings and actions of the Prophet Muhammad, further elaborate on the principles of jihad. For instance, the Prophet Muhammad is reported to have said, "The best jihad is to speak a word of justice to an oppressive ruler." (Sunan Abu Dawood). This Hadith highlights jihad encompasses physical combat but also efforts to uphold justice and morality.

Islamic Jurisprudence and Jihad

Islamic jurisprudence, or fiqh, provides detailed guidelines on the conduct of jihad. Classical Islamic scholars developed extensive legal frameworks to govern the principles and practices of jihad, distinguishing between jihad al-nafs (struggle against one's own self) and jihad al-sayf (military jihad). These legal frameworks outlined the conditions under which jihad can be declared, the conduct during warfare, and the treatment of non-combatants. The concept of jihad, as it is understood by contemporary jihadist groups, often diverges from these traditional interpretations. Jihadists interpret these texts to justify their actions, emphasizing the need for violent struggle against perceived enemies of Islam and the establishment of an Islamic state through force.

Early Islamic Expansion

The notion of jihad has historical roots in the early expansion of the Islamic state. During the Rashidun and Umayyad Caliphates, the Islamic empire expanded through military conquests. This period set a precedent for the idea of a universal Islamic rule, with the caliphs seen as both spiritual and temporal leaders. The desire to spread Islam motivated early expansion efforts and established a political order based on Islamic principles.

Influence of Sayyid Qutb and Abdullah Azzam

In the 20th century, the ideological foundations of global jihad were shaped by figures such as Sayyid Qutb and Abdullah Azzam. Sayyid Qutb, an Egyptian scholar and member of the Muslim Brotherhood, introduced radical ideas about jihad and the need to combat Western influence. His influential work, Milestones, called for a revolutionary struggle against secularism and Western values, framing jihad as a means to purify and transform society.

Abdullah Azzam, a Palestinian scholar and mentor to Osama Bin Laden, further developed the concept of global jihad. Azzam's writings emphasized the importance of jihad as a collective obligation for Muslims and advocated for the establishment of a global Islamic state. His vision rallied fighters from across the Muslim world to join the Afghan resistance against the Soviet invasion.

Rise of Jihadist Movements, Al-Qaeda and the Global Jihad Network

Al-Qaeda, founded by Osama Bin Laden and Abdullah Azzam in 1988, was a major force in formalizing the concept of global jihad. Bin Laden's vision was to create a transnational jihadist network that would unite Muslims under a common cause. Al-Qaeda's organizational structure was designed to facilitate coordination between various jihadist groups and foster a global network of affiliates.

Al-Qaeda's strategy included high-profile attacks intended to provoke a response from Western governments and draw attention to their cause. The group's ideology emphasized the need to strike at the heart of the West to advance the cause of global jihad. The 1998 U.S. Embassy bombings in Kenya and Tanzania, and the 2000 bombing of the USS Cole were key examples of this strategy.

The Emergence of ISIS

The rise of ISIS (Islamic State of Iraq and Syria) marked a significant development in the global jihadist movement. ISIS emerged from Al-Qaeda in Iraq and declared its own caliphate in 2014. The group's extreme tactics and aggressive expansionist agenda drew attention and attracted fighters from around the world.

ISIS's declaration of a caliphate was a bold attempt to revive the historical concept of an Islamic state. The group's brutal enforcement of Sharia law and its systematic persecution of non-Muslims and rival groups exemplified its commitment to establish a global Islamic empire. Although ISIS has lost significant territory, its influence persists through its global network of affiliates and supporters.

Theological Justifications and Strategic Objectives: The Concept of Ummah

The concept of ummah (the global Muslim community) is central to the jihadist vision. Jihadists believe a collective duty to support the establishment of an Islamic State binds all Muslims. This sense of communal responsibility drives their efforts to unite various jihadist factions and coordinate global jihadist activities.

Jihadists argue the current global order, dominated by secular and non-Islamic values, is inherently flawed. They believe true justice and peace can only be achieved through the universal adoption of Islamic principles. This belief motivates their efforts to challenge and overthrow existing political systems and impose their interpretation of Islamic governance.

The Vision of a Global Caliphate

Jihadist groups envision the establishment of a global caliphate as the ultimate goal. A caliphate is an Islamic state led by a caliph, a political and spiritual leader who is considered the successor to the Prophet Muhammad. The idea of a caliphate represents the historical ideal of Islamic governance and serves as a powerful symbol for jihadists.

The pursuit of a global caliphate involves military actions and efforts to influence and recruit supporters worldwide. Jihadist groups use propaganda, social media, and recruitment networks to spread their message and attract followers. Their ability to operate transnationally and maintain ties with various jihadist factions enhances their capacity to coordinate global jihadist efforts.

Al-Qaeda's Role and Alliances

Al-Qaeda continues to play the most significant role in the global jihadist movement. Despite the loss of its original leader, Osama Bin Laden, and the disruption of its operations, the group remains active and influential. Al-Qaeda's strategy includes rebuilding its network, supporting affiliated groups, and conducting attacks to advance its agenda.

The Taliban's resurgence in Afghanistan has provided a new platform for global jihadist activities. The Taliban's alliance with Al-Qaeda and other extremist groups illustrates the convergence of local and global jihadist objectives. This alliance enables Al-Qaeda to leverage the Taliban's influence and resources to further its own goals.

The Challenge of Addressing Global Jihad

Understanding the ideological and theological motivations behind global jihad is crucial for developing effective counterterrorism strategies. The commitment to establish a global Islamic state and enforce Sharia law drives jihadist groups and shapes their actions on the world stage. Addressing the threat posed by global jihad requires a nuanced approach that considers the religious, ideological, and strategic dimensions of the movement.

Global jihad is deeply rooted in Islamic theological concepts and historical precedents. Jihadist groups are driven by a belief in their divine mandate to establish an Islamic state and impose Sharia law globally. Their ideology reflects a vision of global peace achieved through the universal worship of Allah, which influences their actions and strategies. Understanding this context is essential for comprehending the current threat landscape and anticipating the potential impact of future jihadist activities.

Al-Qaeda & the Taliban after 2021

The resurgence of the Taliban and the subsequent takeover of Afghanistan in August 2021 marked a pivotal moment in the global fight against terrorism. This event reshaped the geopolitical landscape of South Asia and reinvigorated the ideological and operational nexus between Al-Qaeda and the Taliban. To understand the current landscape of terrorism, one must examine the profound implications of the Taliban's return to power, the evolving relationship between these two groups, and the strategic shift that has occurred in Afghanistan.

The Taliban's Return to Power: A Historical Context

The Taliban's return to power in 2021 was a direct consequence of decades of conflict, shifting alliances, and evolving strategies within the region. After being ousted from power in 2001 by a U.S.-led coalition following the 9/11 attacks, the Taliban regrouped in Pakistan's tribal areas and slowly regained strength. Over the next two decades, they conducted an insurgency against the Afghan government and coalition forces, exploiting local grievances, tribal dynamics, and regional power vacuums.

By 2020, the U.S. and Taliban entered into negotiations, culminating in the Doha Agreement, which laid out a path for the withdrawal of U.S. and NATO forces in exchange for Taliban guarantees not to allow terrorist groups to operate from Afghan soil. However, the rapid and unplanned withdrawal of U.S. troops, and the collapse of the Afghan government, paved the way for the Taliban to seize control of Kabul on August 15, 2021.

The international community watched in shock as the Taliban swiftly took over the country with minimal resistance. Chaotic scenes at the Kabul Airport, as hundreds of thousands of Afghans desperately sought to flee the country, marked the final days of the Taliban ascension to power. The Taliban's return to power was more than a political and military victory; it represented a major ideological win for Islamist extremists worldwide. For Al-Qaeda, it was a moment of vindication and an opportunity to rebuild and expand its influence.

Al-Qaeda and the Taliban: A Symbiotic Relationship

Al-Qaeda and the Taliban have shared a long-standing relationship that dates to the early 1990s. The bond between the two groups was forged forth on the battlefield during the Afghan-Soviet War, where Osama Bin Laden and other Arab fighters joined Afghan mujahideen to fight against the Soviet forces. This alliance was strengthened by a shared ideological commitment to jihad and a vision of establishing an Islamic emirate governed by Sharia law.

After the Taliban first took control of Afghanistan in 1996, they provided sanctuary to Al-Qaeda, allowing the group to establish training camps and plan operations, including the 9/11 attacks. In return, Al-Qaeda supported the Taliban's fight against the Northern Alliance and provided financial and military support.

The fall of the Taliban in 2001 disrupted this relationship but did not destroy it. Both groups went underground, with Al-Qaeda operatives blending into rural Afghan communities or fleeing to Pakistan, while the Taliban waged a guerrilla war against coalition forces. During this period, Al-Qaeda continued to provide strategic guidance, training, and financial support to the Taliban.

With the Taliban's return to power in 2021, the symbiotic relationship between the two groups renewed. Al-Qaeda sees the Taliban's victory as a vindication of their shared jihadist ideology and as an opportunity to rebuild its capabilities in a safe haven. In return, the Taliban benefit from Al-Qaeda's operational expertise, global network, and propaganda capabilities.

A New Safe Haven for Terrorism

The Taliban's takeover of Afghanistan has transformed the country into a safe haven for terrorist groups once again. Despite the Taliban's assurances in the Doha Agreement to prevent terrorist activities on Afghan soil, the reality on the ground tells a different story. Al-Qaeda, along with other regional and transnational jihadist groups, has taken advantage of the security vacuum created by the Taliban's rise to power.

Reports indicate hundreds of senior Al-Qaeda members have moved back into Afghanistan, particularly in the eastern and southern regions where the Taliban's control is strongest. The presence of Al-Qaeda in these areas is facilitated by the Taliban's network of local fighters, tribal connections, and safe houses established during the insurgency. Al-Qaeda operatives are believed to be embedded within Taliban units, providing training and support while avoiding detection by international intelligence agencies.

Furthermore, the Taliban's victory has inspired jihadist groups worldwide, including those affiliated with Al-Qaeda in the Arabian Peninsula (AQAP), Al-Qaeda in the Islamic Maghreb (AQIM), and Hayat Tahrir al-Sham in Syria. These groups view the Taliban's success as proof that jihadist ideologies can triumph over Western powers, providing a morale boost and a recruitment tool.

The Taliban's control of Afghanistan also provides a strategic advantage for Al-Qaeda, as the group can now operate with greater freedom and less risk of drone strikes or special operations raids. The vast and rugged terrain of Afghanistan, coupled with a weakened Afghan intelligence network, makes it easier for Al-Qaeda to plan, coordinate, and launch operations against Western targets.

The Taliban's Internal Dynamics and Its Impact on Al-Qaeda

Understanding the relationship between the Taliban and Al-Qaeda requires an examination of the internal dynamics within the Taliban movement itself. The Taliban is not a monolithic entity but rather a coalition of various factions and networks, each with its own leaders, agendas, and ideologies.

The two most prominent factions within the Taliban are the Kandahari Taliban, led by Hibatullah Akhundzada, and the Haqqani Network, led by Sirajuddin Haqqani. While both factions share a commitment to jihad and the establishment of an Islamic emirate, there are differences in their strategic priorities and relationships with Al-Qaeda.

The Kandahari Taliban, based in southern Afghanistan, are primarily focused on consolidating their control over Afghanistan and establishing a stable government based on their interpretation of Sharia law.

This faction is seen as more nationalistic and less inclined to engage in transnational jihadist activities. On the other hand, the Haqqani Network, which operates primarily in eastern Afghanistan and Pakistan, has a more global jihadist outlook. The Haqqani Network has long-standing ties to Al-Qaeda and has been involved in numerous attacks against Western and Afghan forces, including the 2008 attack on the Indian Embassy in Kabul and the 2011 attack on the U.S. Embassy.

The Haqqani Network's leadership has always been more open to collaborating with Al-Qaeda, providing them with safe havens and logistical support. This faction's influence within the Taliban government has grown significantly since the takeover, with Sirajuddin Haqqani serving as the acting interior minister, controlling the police and security forces in Afghanistan. This position gives the Haqqani Network considerable power to shape Afghanistan's security policies and its relationship with Al-Qaeda.

The interplay between these factions has significant implications for Al-Qaeda's operations in Afghanistan. While the Kandahari Taliban may be more focused on domestic governance, the Haqqani Network's influence ensures that Al-Qaeda continues to have a foothold in the country. This dynamic allows Al-Qaeda to operate freely while maintaining a low profile to avoid attracting international attention.

It has to be mentioned that Al-Qaeda gave their pledge of allegiance to Haibatullah Akhundzada, and he was the one who organized the Jigra that selected the new Al-Qaeda leadership. So, the relation between Kandahari Taliban is just as important to them as the close relation to the Haqqani Network.

Al-Qaeda's Strategic Shift: A Focus on Afghanistan

With the Taliban back in power, Al-Qaeda has undergone a strategic shift, prioritizing Afghanistan as its primary base of operations. This shift reflects a return to the group's roots and recognition of the strategic value of Afghanistan as a staging ground for jihadist activities. Al-Qaeda's current strategy in Afghanistan focuses on three key objectives:

1. Rebuilding Capabilities: Al-Qaeda is using Afghanistan as a safe haven to rebuild its operational capabilities, including training camps, recruitment networks, and financial infrastructure. The group leverages its relationship with the Taliban to access resources and establish bases in remote areas of the country.

2. Regional Expansion: Al-Qaeda aims to use Afghanistan as a springboard to expand its influence in the broader region, particularly in Central Asia, South Asia, and the Middle East. The group is actively recruiting fighters from neighboring countries and fostering alliances with local jihadist groups.

3. Global Outreach: Al-Qaeda continues to pursue its long-term goal of global jihad, seeking to inspire and coordinate attacks against Western targets. The group's propaganda efforts have intensified since the Taliban's takeover, with Al-Qaeda's media wing, As-Sahab, releasing a steady stream of videos, statements, and publications celebrating the Taliban's victory and calling for attacks against Western interests.

International Implications and the Way Forward

The Taliban's takeover of Afghanistan and the resurgence of Al-Qaeda have profound implications for global security. The reestablishment of a jihadist safe haven in Afghanistan poses a direct threat to the United States, Europe, and other Western nations. Al-Qaeda's ability to plan, coordinate, and execute attacks from Afghan soil will lead to a new wave of terrorism, reminiscent of the pre-9/11 era.

To address this threat, the international community must adopt a multi-faceted approach that includes intelligence sharing, targeted counterterrorism operations, and diplomatic engagement with regional powers. It is crucial to disrupt Al-Qaeda's networks, cut off its funding sources, and prevent the group from exploiting Afghanistan as a launchpad for global jihad.

Additionally, there is a need to support local actors within Afghanistan who are opposed to both the Taliban and Al-Qaeda. The biggest example being the National Resistance Front of Afghanistan under the command of Ahmad Massoud, the son of the legend and former leader of the Northern Alliance Ahmad Shah Massoud. He was killed by Al-Qaeda two days before 9/11. The front has both a political wing and an armed wing. The armed forces of the NRF are led by former Special Forces Commander Khalid Amiry who went to Panjshir Province right after the fall of Kabul. He took with him a group of several hundred soldiers who all joined Massoud's NRF.

Another major resistance group is the Afghanistan Freedom Front, led by former General Yasin Zia. This front is very active, works closely together with the National Resistance Front and consists, just like the NRF, of Afghan National Army operatives, former Special Forces units and NDS staff.

Those two major resistance forces are the people we, the West, trained, and they are fighting the Taliban on a daily basis. Since August 15th 2021, they have killed and injured over 4.000 Taliban in hundreds of directed attacks.

Building the capacity of Afghan resistance groups create a counterbalance to jihadist influence and promote stability in the region.

Inside Al-Qaeda

Al-Qaeda has undergone significant transformations in its leadership and structure since its inception in the late 1980s. Originally formed as a base for jihadists committed to fighting Soviet forces in Afghanistan, Al-Qaeda has evolved into a global terrorist organization with a complex and adaptive network. Over the years, the leadership and organizational structure of Al-Qaeda have shifted to reflect strategic changes, geographic priorities, and responses to external pressures - particularly those from Western and regional intelligence agencies. A comprehensive understanding of Al-Qaeda's current leadership and organizational structure is crucial for grasping the group's continued resilience and the ongoing threat it poses to global security.

The Evolution of Al-Qaeda's Leadership

The leadership of Al-Qaeda has always been central to its ideology, strategy, and operations. Osama Bin Laden, along with Abdullah Azzam and other militants, founded Al-Qaeda in the late 1980s with the aim of creating a vanguard for global jihad. Bin Laden's ability to unite disparate jihadist factions under a common cause, combined with his financial resources and charisma, was instrumental in Al-Qaeda's early prominence.

Osama Bin Laden's Leadership (1988-2011)

Osama Bin Laden led Al-Qaeda from its founding in 1988 until his death in 2011. Under his leadership, Al-Qaeda transformed from a loosely connected network of jihadists into a structured organization capable of executing large-scale terrorist attacks. Bin Laden's vision of global jihad, particularly targeting the "far enemy" — the United States and its allies — culminated in the September 11, 2001, attacks. These attacks marked a significant turning point for both Al-Qaeda and global counterterrorism efforts, prompting the U.S.-led invasion of Afghanistan and the dismantling of the Taliban regime, which had been providing safe haven to Al-Qaeda.

After the invasion, Bin Laden went into hiding in Pakistan, where he continued to influence Al-Qaeda's strategy and operations through a network of couriers. Despite losing its base in Afghanistan, Al-Qaeda adapted by decentralizing its operations, encouraging regional affiliates to conduct attacks while maintaining a unified ideological framework. Bin Laden's death in a U.S. Navy SEAL raid in Abbottabad, Pakistan, in 2011 was a significant blow to Al-Qaeda but did not spell the end of the organization.

Ayman al-Zawahiri's Tenure (2011-2022)

Following Bin Laden's death, Ayman al-Zawahiri, an Egyptian jihadist and former leader of Egyptian Islamic Jihad, took over as the leader of Al-Qaeda. Zawahiri's tenure was marked by both continuity and adaptation. While he maintained Bin Laden's vision of global jihad, he also oversaw a period of further decentralization.

Zawahiri's leadership style differed significantly from Bin Laden's. Whereas Bin Laden was known for his charismatic leadership, Zawahiri was seen as more doctrinal and ideological, focusing heavily on providing religious justification for Al-Qaeda's actions. Under Zawahiri, Al-Qaeda sought to rebuild its capabilities, expand its network of affiliates, and exploit regional conflicts to establish footholds in ungoverned or unstable areas. However, Zawahiri was less successful in uniting the global jihadist movement, particularly after the emergence of the Islamic State (ISIS), which declared its caliphate in 2014 and directly challenged Al-Qaeda's leadership of the global jihadist movement.

Leadership Changes in 2022

In 2022, a U.S, drone strike in Kabul Afghanistan killed Ayman Al-Zawahiri, marking another significant turning point for Al-Qaeda. For a short period of time, Saif Al-Adl, who returned from Iran to Kabul, took over the scepter. Following Zawahiri's death, a significant shift in leadership took place, orchestrated under the auspices of the Taliban's leader, Hibatullah Akhundzada.

The Jirga of 2022: A Turning Point

After the killing of al-Zawahiri, Akhundzada, the Taliban supreme leader, organized a jirga, a traditional assembly of leaders and elders, to address the leadership vacuum in Al-Qaeda. A jirga is a crucial cultural mechanism in Afghan society, used for decision-making and conflict resolution. It involves a gathering of tribal elders, religious scholars, and other influential figures to discuss and resolve matters of significant importance. In this context, the jirga held in 2022 was an extraordinary event that brought together the senior leaders of Al-Qaeda's Shura Council and all leaders of the international affiliates and Al-Qaeda branches to deliberate on the organization's future leadership.

During this jirga, significant decisions were made regarding Al-Qaeda's leadership. Contrary to many expectations, Saif al-Adel, a long-time senior figure in Al-Qaeda and a former Egyptian special forces officer, was not selected as the new leader. Many within the Shura Council were reluctant to have him take over as the Emir, preferring to pass leadership to a younger generation.

New Leadership Under Hamza, Saad and Abdallah Bin Laden

Instead of Saif al-Adel, the Shura Council chose Hamza Bin Laden, Osama Bin Laden's son, as the new Emir of Al-Qaeda. Despite reports Hamza had been killed in a U.S. drone strike, he survived and returned to Afghanistan from Pakistan in 2022. His return coincided with the wedding of his brother, Saad Bin Ladon, who had also been presumed dead but had survived and returned to Kandahar from Iran in 2021.

Hamza Bin Laden's appointment as the new Emir marked a generational shift in Al-Qaeda's leadership. Saad Bin Laden was named deputy Emir, while Abdallah Bin Laden, Osama's eldest son, was appointed third in line. The presence of the Bin Laden family at the highest levels of Al-Qaeda's leadership underscores a return to the organization's roots and a focus on leveraging the Bin Laden name for recruitment and propaganda.

This information, based on Human Intelligence (HUMINT) sources close to the organization, confirmed by the former Afghan Intelligence apparatus and its leaders, was corroborated by individuals who attended Saad's wedding. These sources independently verified that Hamza and Saad were alive and in good health at the event, further solidifying the credibility of these reports. In a later stage, other sources revealed they had seen Hamza Bin Laden in Panjshir Province. One source confirmed that Hamza was at Mullah Omar's house in Kandahar in 2022 and one source confirmed Hamza visiting Kabul. In total, we had eight eyewitnesses confirmed Hamza Bin Laden was alive and in Afghanistan.

Al-Qaeda's Current Leadership Structure

The new leadership structure under Hamza Bin Laden reflects a blend of continuity and change. While Al-Qaeda continues to pursue its long-standing goals of global jihad, the inclusion of Bin Laden's sons in key leadership roles signals a potential shift towards revitalizing the organization's brand and appeal among younger jihadists.

Key Figures in Al-Qaeda's Leadership

- Hamza Bin Laden: As the new Emir of Al-Qaeda, Hamza Bin Laden is expected to uphold his father's legacy while also addressing the new challenges facing the organization. Known for his vocal condemnations of the West and calls for attacks against U.S. interests, Hamza's leadership is likely to focus on reinvigorating Al-Qaeda's global jihadist narrative.

- Saad Bin Laden: As deputy Emir, Saad Bin Laden brings a wealth of experience from his time in Iran and Afghanistan. His role is expected to support Hamza in both strategic and operational capacities, ensuring the coherence of Al-Qaeda's global network.

- Abdallah Bin Laden: Third in line, Abdallah Bin Laden is poised to play a critical role in maintaining the Bin Laden legacy within Al-Qaeda. His position within the leadership structure reinforces the organization's continuity and its commitment to the vision laid out by Osama Bin Laden.

The Heavy Impact of Hamza Bin Laden's Appointment as Al-Qaeda Emir

The appointment of Hamza Bin Laden as the new Emir of Al-Qaeda represents a pivotal moment for the organization and the broader international jihadist community. Hamza's ascension is more than a mere succession; it marks a strategic consolidation of power and a significant shift in the dynamics of global jihadism. His leadership is poised to have profound implications for both Al-Qaeda and its relationship with other jihadist factions, particularly in the context of the broader vision to establish a unified caliphate.

The Symbolic and Strategic Significance of Hamza Bin Laden

Hamza Bin Laden's appointment as the Emir of Al-Qaeda carries considerable symbolic weight. As the son of Osama Bin Laden, Hamza inherits a position of leadership and a powerful legacy which resonates deeply within jihadist circles. His leadership rejuvenates Al-Qaeda's brand, connects the organization to its foundational roots, and reinforces its claims to legitimacy within the jihadist movement.

Hamza Bin Laden's appointment is a masterstroke in propaganda. The Bin Laden name remains one of the most potent symbols in jihadist rhetoric, and Hamza's leadership will likely amplify Al-Qaeda's appeal among potential recruits and sympathizers. His association with the Bin Laden family reinforces the narrative of Al-Qaeda as the true heir to Osama Bin Laden's vision, differentiating it from rival groups like ISIS. The revival of the Bin Laden name at the helm of Al-Qaeda serves to inspire existing followers, rally new recruits, and enhance the group's prestige in the global jihadist arena.

Strategically, Hamza's leadership signals a period of consolidation and renewed focus for Al-Qaeda. His role as Emir will likely involve steering the organization towards greater unity and operational coherence. By positioning himself as a central figure, Hamza is expected to strengthen Al-Qaeda's network of affiliates, improve coordination between regional branches, and reinvigorate the group's global strategy. This consolidation is crucial for countering the challenges posed by other jihadist factions and sustaining Al-Qaeda's influence in the face of shifting dynamics within the global jihadist movement.

Impact on the International Jihadi Community

The international jihadist community is poised to experience a significant shift with Hamza Bin Laden's rise to leadership. His appointment is likely to influence several aspects of the global jihadist landscape.

Hamza's leadership is expected to accelerate efforts to forge stronger alliances and coalitions within the jihadist community. Under his guidance, Al-Qaeda is likely to pursue more aggressive outreach to other jihadist groups, including those which have historically been rivals or independent actors. The goal will be to create a more cohesive global jihadist network united by a common objective: the establishment of a vast caliphate under unified leadership.

One of Hamza's strategic priorities will be to strengthen ties with other influential jihadist groups. This includes building on existing relationships and forging new alliances with organizations such as the Taliban, Al-Shabaab, and various Salafi-jihadist factions across the Middle East, North Africa, and South Asia. By presenting a unified front, Hamza aims to consolidate jihadist efforts and resources, enhancing their collective impact and strategic positioning.

Hamza's leadership is likely to have a significant impact on recruitment and mobilization within the jihadist community. His appointment will be used to galvanize support among existing followers and attract new recruits who are inspired by the legacy of the Bin Laden family. This increase in recruitment could potentially bolster Al-Qaeda's operational capabilities and expand its influence in regions where it seeks to establish a stronger foothold.

Hamza Bin Laden's appointment is also expected to enhance strategic synergies with Sirajuddin Haqqani, the leader of the Haqqani Network and a key figure within the Taliban. Both Haqqani and Hamza are aligned in their vision of a unified jihadist front, and their collaboration is anticipated to have a profound impact on the broader jihadist agenda.

A major objective of Hamza Bin Laden and Sirajuddin Haqqani is the establishment of a large caliphate under a unified leadership. Haqqani, who wields considerable influence within the Taliban and among other jihadist factions, is positioned as the potential Caliph. The collaboration between Hamza and Haqqani aims to create a comprehensive jihadist coalition that encompasses various groups and factions, all working towards the goal of a single, expansive caliphate.

The Taliban's control over Afghanistan provides a critical base for Al-Qaeda's operations and for the realization of their joint objectives. Under Haqqani's influence, the Taliban has demonstrated a commitment to providing a safe haven for Al-Qaeda and other allied groups. This alliance is instrumental in facilitating the movement of fighters, resources, and operational planning across regions, thus supporting the broader jihadist goal of establishing a caliphate.

The partnership between Hamza Bin Laden and Sirajuddin Haqqani is expected to result in more coordinated operations and aligned strategic goals. This includes joint military operations, coordinated propaganda efforts, and synchronized attacks designed to further the cause of global jihad. Their combined efforts will likely focus on destabilizing regions of strategic importance, undermining Western interests, and building a global jihadist network capable of challenging established power structures.

The collaboration between Al-Qaeda and the Taliban under Hamza and Haqqani's leadership is poised to increase the influence and power of their respective groups. By uniting their resources and capabilities, they aim to project strength and authority within the jihadist movement and beyond. This consolidation of power is intended to solidify their leadership, expand their reach, and enhance their ability to execute high-impact operations.

Hamza Bin Laden's appointment as Al-Qaeda's Emir represents a transformative shift in the global jihadist landscape. His leadership, coupled with strategic partnerships such as the one with Sirajuddin Haqqani, is set to redefine the dynamics of jihadist alliances and operations. The impact of this new leadership will likely be profound, influencing recruitment, operational strategies, and the broader vision of establishing a unified caliphate.

As Al-Qaeda continues to evolve under Hamza's guidance, its ability to shape and influence the global jihadist movement will be a critical factor in determining the future trajectory of international terrorism.

The Global Network, uniting all affiliated terrorist Groups

The rise of Al-Qaeda and its integration with the Taliban has led to an unprecedented expansion of their training and operational capacities. The current landscape of Al-Qaeda's influence and operational scope represents a significant shift from the pre-9/11 era, reflecting a more robust and interconnected jihadist network. This chapter examines the details of Al-Qaeda's extensive training network, its impact on global jihadism, and the imminent threat posed by the convergence of numerous jihadist groups under a unified agenda.

Expansion of Training Camps

Since the fall of Kabul in August 2021, the strategic environment in Afghanistan has dramatically shifted. Under the leadership of Sirajuddin Haqqani and with Al-Qaeda's active involvement, a sprawling network of over 40 training camps has been established across the country. These camps serve as crucial hubs for the indoctrination, training, and operational preparation of a diverse array of jihadist groups.

The training camps are used by Al-Qaeda to train a wide range of affiliated and allied groups. These include:

- Al-Qaeda core members (AQ)
- Al-Qaeda in the Arabian Peninsula (AQAP)
- Al-Qaeda in the Islamic Maghreb (AQIM)

- Al-Qaeda in the Sinai Peninsula (AQSP)
- Al-Qaeda in the Indian Subcontinent (AQIS)
- Boko Haram
- Jama'at Nasr al-Islam wal-Muslimin (JNIM)
- Islamic Jihad Union (IJU)
- Katibat al-Tawhid wal-Jihad (KTJ)
- Islamic Movement of Uzbekistan (IMU)
- Tahrir al-Sham (TAS)
- Ansar al-Din
- Ansar al-Islam
- Ansar al-Sharia
- Hurras al-Din
- Al-Shabaab
- Turkistan Islamic Party (TIP)
- Jaish-e-Mohammed (JeM)
- Lashkar-e-Jhangvi (LeJ)
- Tehrik-i-Taliban (TTP)
- Lashkar-e-Taiba (LET)
- Islamic State Khorasan Province (ISKP)
- Balochistan Liberation Army (BLA)
- Hamas
- Hezbollah

These camps provide comprehensive training programs, including weapons handling, urban warfare, guerrilla tactics, and indoctrination in extremist ideologies. The extensive scope of this training network underscores Al-Qaeda's ambition to cultivate a formidable cadre of fighters capable of executing complex operations on a global scale.

A notable development in this training network is the takeover of the Islamic State Khorasan Province (ISKP) by the Haqqani Network (and thus by Al-Qaeda). Previously an ISIS affiliate, ISKP's leadership has been restructured under the influence of Sirajuddin Haqqani. The current leader Sanaullah Ghafari, appointed by Haqqani, is a member of the Haqqani network. This takeover signifies a strategic consolidation of power and an effort to unify the jihadist front under a single leadership structure.

Growth and Capacity of Al-Qaeda compared to the pre-9/11 situation

The expansion of Al-Qaeda's training camps is paralleled by a dramatic increase in the organization's size and capabilities. Comparing the pre-9/11 period to the present reveals stark contrasts in terms of scale and operational capacity.

Prior to September 11, 2001, Al-Qaeda operated a limited number of training camps in Afghanistan. In contrast, the current network comprises over 30 camps, reflecting a significant expansion in both geographical reach and operational scope.

This proliferation of training facilities allows Al-Qaeda to accommodate a larger number of recruits and to train them more intensively, contributing to the organization's increased capabilities. Each camp houses around 1,000 trainees. The worst part: these camps are almost all situated in former US and ISAF bases.

In the pre-9/11 era, Al-Qaeda trained approximately 50,000 fighters over a span of more than a decade. In the recent period, however, the organization has trained between 70,000 and 85,000 fighters in less than three years. This surge in training capacity underscores Al-Qaeda's commitment to building a substantial and effective fighting force.

The number of Al-Qaeda members in Afghanistan has also seen a dramatic increase. Before 9/11, Al-Qaeda had approximately 4,800 members in Afghanistan. Between 2016 and 2021, this number grew to approximately 12,000, reflecting the organization's growing influence and operational capacity. In 2024, Al-Qaeda's ranks have expanded to over 16,000 fighters. This growth is partly attributable to the organization's role in the Taliban's resurgence and its strategic positioning in the country.

Al-Qaeda's integration with the Taliban has deepened through various means, including the provision of security services and the establishment of collaborative networks. The presence of Al-Qaeda members in key Taliban security positions highlights the close relationship between the two groups. Al-Qaeda now functions as a job agency for affiliated groups, providing training, equipment, and operational support to new recruits from Europe, Asia, and the Middle East.

Implications for the Global Jihadist Movement

The convergence of Al-Qaeda's expanded training network and its strategic alliances with other jihadist groups has significant implications for the global jihadist movement.

The extensive training network and the strategic consolidation under Haqqani's leadership are indicative of a broader effort to unify diverse jihadist factions. Groups with historically divergent goals and ideologies are now joining forces under a common agenda: the establishment of a global caliphate. This unification transcends traditional sectarian divides with Sunni and Shia differences being temporarily set aside in pursuit of a shared goal.

The imminent large-scale attack on the US and Europe, as described in this book, will mark the beginning of a true global jihad. The unification of jihadist groups under Al-Qaeda and the Taliban represents a significant escalation in the jihadist movement's capabilities and ambitions. The coordinated efforts of these groups are aimed at creating a caliphate that encompasses vast territories and unites diverse jihadist factions under a single leadership.

Iran's Role in Supporting Al-Qaeda

Iran's involvement in supporting Al-Qaeda, while complex and often shrouded in ambiguity, plays a significant role in the broader jihadist landscape. Despite the sectarian differences between Iran's Shia leadership and Al-Qaeda's Sunni extremists, Iran has strategically engaged with various elements of Al-Qaeda for mutual benefit. This chapter explores Iran's role in harboring key Al-Qaeda figures, facilitating their movements, and supporting their operational activities across the globe.

One of the most contentious aspects of Iran's relationship with Al-Qaeda is its role in providing sanctuary to high-profile Al-Qaeda members. Following the U.S.-led invasion of Afghanistan and the subsequent pressure on Al-Qaeda, Iran became a pivotal refuge for numerous individuals linked to the organization.

In the aftermath of the U.S. invasion of Afghanistan and the fall of the Taliban regime, several senior Al-Qaeda members sought refuge in Iran. Among them were prominent figures such as Saif al-Adl, a key military commander and strategist for Al-Qaeda, and members of the Bin Laden family, including Saad Bin Laden, who had previously been thought to be dead.

- Saif al-Adl: Saif al-Adl, who was considered one of Al-Qaeda's most senior operatives, was sheltered by Iran for several years. His presence in Iran was a closely guarded secret, reflecting the complex interplay of geopolitics and jihadist strategies. Saif al-Adl's stay in Iran highlights the extent of Tehran's engagement with Al-Qaeda, despite the group's Sunni orientation and the Shia-Sunni divide.

- Saad Bin Laden: Saad Bin Laden, one of Osama Bin Laden's sons, also found sanctuary in Iran. Contrary to earlier reports of his death, Saad Bin Laden was located in Iran, where he continued to contribute to Al-Qaeda's operations. His presence was confirmed by HUMINT sources and underscored Iran's role in providing a haven for key Al-Qaeda figures.

- Other Bin Laden Family Members: The Bin Laden family, notably including Abdullah Bin Laden, was also sheltered in Iran. Their protection in Iran further indicates Tehran's willingness to engage with Al-Qaeda's leadership, despite the potential repercussions of such alliances.

Iran's strategic position has also allowed it to play a crucial role in facilitating the movement of Al-Qaeda operatives between different conflict zones. This logistical support has significantly enhanced Al-Qaeda's ability to operate across multiple regions. Iran's geographical location has made it a key transit hub for Al-Qaeda operatives traveling between Afghanistan and Pakistan. This route has been crucial for maintaining operational continuity and facilitating the movement of personnel, resources, and strategic directives between these regions.

Beyond Afghanistan and Pakistan, Iran has provided logistical support that enables Al-Qaeda operatives to travel to other major jihadist theaters. Al-Qaeda operatives have been able to transit through Iran to reach conflict zones in Iraq and Syria. This support has allowed for the movement of fighters and resources into the heart of the Syrian civil war and the Iraqi insurgency, bolstering Al-Qaeda's presence and influence in these critical areas. The movement of Al-Qaeda operatives to Yemen has been facilitated by Iran, contributing to the establishment of Al-Qaeda in the Arabian Peninsula (AQAP). Yemen's ongoing conflict and instability have made it a strategic focal point for Al-Qaeda's operations, with Iran's support playing a key role in sustaining AQAP's activities. Iran's influence extends to Africa, where it has supported Al-Qaeda's affiliates in Somalia and across East and West Africa. The facilitation of travel and support to groups like Al-Shabaab has enabled these affiliates to strengthen their operations and expand their reach across the continent.

Iran's involvement extends beyond mere sanctuary; it has actively facilitated the free movement of Al-Qaeda operatives by providing logistical support, including false documentation and safe passage through its territory. This logistical network has been instrumental in enabling Al-Qaeda to operate on a global scale, circumventing the restrictive measures imposed by counterterrorism efforts. Iran's support for Al-Qaeda, despite their differing sectarian affiliations, can be understood through a lens of strategic interest and geopolitical calculation.

Iran has historically pursued strategic alliances with various militant groups to counterbalance U.S. and Western influence in the Middle East. By supporting Al-Qaeda, Iran has sought to extend its influence and undermine its regional rivals, including the U.S., Israel, and Sunni Gulf states. The support for Al-Qaeda also aligns with Iran's broader strategy of proxy warfare. By providing sanctuary and facilitating the movement of Al-Qaeda operatives, Iran leverages these relationships to extend its geopolitical reach and support its regional objectives.

While Iran's support for Sunni Al-Qaeda operatives may appear contradictory, it reflects a pragmatic approach to achieving strategic objectives. Iran's support for Al-Qaeda is a calculated decision to achieve strategic goals, even at the cost of sectarian harmony.

Legacy of Osama Bin Laden's Plan

The current state of Al-Qaeda and its operations can be viewed as a direct manifestation of Osama Bin Laden's larger strategic vision, often referred to as the "7 Stages Towards a Caliphate" plan. This plan outlines a series of phases aimed at establishing a global caliphate through a combination of militant activities, strategic alliances, and political maneuvers as we described in the previous chapter.

The expansion of Al-Qaeda's training network, the consolidation of jihadist factions, and the strategic leadership shifts all align with the goals outlined in Bin Laden's plan. The current trajectory of Al-Qaeda and its affiliates reflects the ongoing implementation of Bin Laden's vision, with the aim of achieving a unified caliphate that spans multiple regions and incorporates various jihadist groups.

The evolution of Al-Qaeda from its pre-9/11 state to its current capabilities underscores the effectiveness of Bin Laden's strategic planning. The expansion of training camps, the growth in membership, and the unification of jihadist factions are all elements of a carefully orchestrated strategy aimed at achieving long-term objectives in the global jihadist movement.

The transformation of Al-Qaeda and its integration with the Taliban represent a new era of jihadist consolidation and expansion. The establishment of an extensive training network, the unification of diverse jihadist factions, and the implementation of Bin Laden's strategic vision all point to a significantly enhanced threat to global security.

As these groups prepare for coordinated actions and large-scale attacks, the implications for international stability and counterterrorism efforts become increasingly critical. The coming global jihad represents a profound challenge to existing security frameworks and underscores the urgent need for a comprehensive and strategic response.

Unveiling the Plot

The HUMINT efforts that discovered the Plot

The discovery of the plot which forms the core of this book was not an accident. It was the result of meticulous Human Intelligence (HUMINT) operations that spanned three years and involved a network of dedicated and highly skilled operatives who infiltrated various levels of the Al-Qaeda and Taliban structures. This chapter delves into the complexities and intricacies of these efforts, highlighting the challenges and triumphs that led to uncovering one of the most significant threats in recent history.

The Foundations of HUMINT Operations

Human Intelligence, or HUMINT, is the collection of information from human sources. In the context of counterterrorism, it involves deploying operatives, cultivating informants, and leveraging local assets to gather actionable intelligence. The effectiveness of HUMINT relies heavily on the trust and relationships built between intelligence officers and their sources. In regions like Afghanistan and Pakistan, where tribal affiliations, personal loyalties, and cultural nuances play crucial roles, building such trust is an incredibly delicate and time-consuming process.

After the fall of Kabul in August 2021, the urgency to gather intelligence on Al-Qaeda and Taliban activities in Afghanistan increased dramatically. The withdrawal of Western forces created a vacuum, not only in terms of security but also in intelligence-gathering capabilities. Recognizing this gap made us intensify our HUMINT operations, recruiting new assets and reactivating dormant networks.

This was needed because the agencies stopped doing this, and in many cases were not trusted anymore by the Afghan's who felt betrayed. The simple reason why we managed to build a large network of trusted sources lies in the fact that we were contacted by former informants and former military- and intelligence operatives who needed help. Regardless of the promises our nations made to them, they were left alone with their families. We took over the task of making sure they had food, safe-houses, and the right support to keep them safe from the Taliban.

This situation created a foundation of strong trust between us and our friends in Afghanistan. These individuals helped us in return for the help we gave to them and their families.

Infiltration and Source Development

The success of the HUMINT efforts can be attributed to a network of informants who were able to embed themselves within the fabric of Afghan society. These operatives, many of whom had deep cultural and linguistic ties to the region, gained the trust of key figures within the Taliban and Al-Qaeda.

The recruitment of sources strategically targeted individuals who had access to sensitive information - this included former government officials, disillusioned Taliban fighters who were not paid by their leadership, and even members of the Haqqani network who were dissatisfied with the group's direction under Sirajuddin Haqqani.

One of the key challenges in this process was to identify and approach individuals who were both willing and capable of providing credible intelligence. The operatives employed a range of tactics to achieve this, from leveraging personal relationships to exploiting rivalries within and between terrorist organizations. For instance, the intense competition between different factions within the Taliban often provided opportunities to cultivate sources who were eager to undermine their rivals.

Breaking into the Inner Circles

The most critical breakthrough in uncovering the plot came from successfully infiltrating the inner circles of Al-Qaeda and the Taliban leadership. This was no small feat, given the layers of security and loyalty surrounding figures like Hamza Bin Laden and Sirajuddin Haqqani.

Operatives had to navigate a complex web of personal guards, tribal loyalties, and religious obligations to even get close to these individuals.

The primary sources of intelligence are persons who are close to the Bin Laden's who decided to cooperate with us. These sources provided invaluable information about the internal dynamics of the Taliban leadership and their connections with Al-Qaeda. Their insights into the preparations for a major attack on Western targets were instrumental in focusing the efforts of HUMINT operatives on uncovering the specifics of the plot. They sent us detailed information and photographs of the locations (a GDI, Taliban Intelligence, safe-house) in Kandahar where the Bin Ladens are housed. We knew from day-to-day where Hamza and Saad Bin Laden would be.

The Role of Technology in HUMINT Operations

While HUMINT is traditionally viewed as a human-centric endeavor, technology has increasingly played a significant role in modern intelligence operations. In this case, technological tools supported and enhanced the HUMINT efforts. Encrypted communications, geolocation tracking, and data analytics corroborated information provided by human sources and monitored movements of key individuals.

For example, we provided tools - for security reasons we will not describe what kind of tools - to support the information received from our HUMINT sources. This blend of traditional HUMINT with cutting-edge technology allowed us to piece together the puzzle of the plot in a way which would not have been possible using either method in isolation.

Another very important part of uncovering the plot is the use of our basic knowledge about Al-Qaeda over the past 20 years. The plans that were found in these twenty years and the publications As-Sahab and the other Media-wings from Al-Qaeda made public to their followers.

Navigating the Dangers

Operating in a hostile environment like Afghanistan poses numerous risks for HUMINT sources. Several sources involved in these efforts faced extreme dangers, with some even paying the ultimate price for their bravery.

The danger is not limited to the sources alone. Their families and associates also faced significant risks. In one case, a source who provided critical information about a training camp was forced to flee with his family to a neighboring country after his identity was compromised. His willingness to continue providing intelligence from exile underscored the deep commitment many sources had to the cause of countering terrorism.

The Breakthrough: Uncovering the Plot

The culmination of these efforts came when a network of sources reported simultaneous unusual activities across several Al-Qaeda and Taliban camps. This included increased communications, the movement of operatives across borders, and the assembly of key leaders. We connected these activities to a coordinated plan for an attack targeting multiple Western cities.

Crucial pieces of intelligence came from high-level meetings attended by Taliban Leaders, leaders from the Haqqani network, and senior Al-Qaeda members. During meetings, some of the details of the plot were discussed including the logistics of the operation and the expected impact. The information was relayed to us within hours. We simply connected the dots. When we combined this information with the huge amount of information already obtained the plan became clearer and clearer.

The Real Value of HUMINT Versus OSINT

In the world of intelligence, not all methods are created equal. While Open Source Intelligence (OSINT) has gained significant popularity in recent years, especially with the rise of digital media and the internet, it is important to understand its limitations compared to the power of Human Intelligence (HUMINT).

OSINT involves collecting information from publicly available sources such as news articles, social media, government reports, and other open platforms. In contrast, HUMINT relies on human sources and interactions to gather secret or classified information that is not available to the general public.

While OSINT can be useful in some contexts, it is often viewed as "child's play" in the eyes of seasoned intelligence professionals who understand the complexities and nuances of uncovering plots and threats. Our discovery of the Al-Qaeda plot serves as a compelling example of why HUMINT remains the gold standard for serious intelligence work.

The Limitations of OSINT

Anyone with internet access and basic analytical skills can engage in OSINT activities. It's widely used by journalists, researchers, and amateur sleuths to gather information and build narratives. However, this accessibility is also its greatest limitation. Because OSINT relies on information that is publicly available, it is inherently reactive. It deals with information that is already out in the open, which means that any adversary who is even remotely cautious will avoid leaving traces that can be picked up by OSINT methods.

Furthermore, OSINT lacks the depth and nuance required to understand the intentions, motivations, and plans of terrorist organizations like Al-Qaeda. Terrorists are aware of the capabilities of OSINT practitioners and often employ various tactics to mislead, deceive, or overwhelm open-source analysts with false or misleading information. This creates a significant challenge for anyone attempting to rely solely on OSINT to uncover actionable intelligence.

Unlike OSINT, HUMINT is proactive. It involves embedding operatives and cultivating sources within organizations of interest. These sources can provide unique insights that are simply unattainable through open-source methods. HUMINT allows intelligence operatives to penetrate the inner workings of terrorist cells, understand their hierarchies, gain insights into their planning processes, and, most importantly, uncover plots before they are executed.

The value of HUMINT is particularly evident in environments where information is tightly controlled, such as within Al-Qaeda's leadership or the Taliban's inner circle. Here, secrets are closely guarded, and communications are carefully monitored to avoid leaks. HUMINT operatives, by building trust and leveraging personal relationships, can gain access to information that would never be shared on open platforms.

For example, in uncovering the plot we discuss here, HUMINT sources were able to attend high-level meetings, overhear sensitive conversations, and gain access to information that detailed the plans for a coordinated attack on Western cities. None of this information would have been accessible through OSINT, which is confined to what is already public.

While OSINT has its place in the intelligence community, it is often overrated by those who do not understand the deeper layers of intelligence gathering. OSINT is useful for understanding broad trends, analyzing public sentiment, and identifying potential threats after they have manifested. It can provide context and supplement other forms of intelligence like HUMINT or SIGINT but is rarely sufficient on its own to uncover serious plots or prevent attacks before they occur.

Thousands of individuals, from journalists to social media analysts, engage in OSINT daily sifting through the vast amounts of information available on the internet. This has led to a perception that OSINT is a quick and easy way to gather intelligence. However, this overlooks the most critical information. Details about upcoming attacks, the identities of key operatives, and the locations of safe houses cannot be found on Google or Twitter. They are hidden behind layers of secrecy and deception, accessible only through the painstaking work of HUMINT operatives who risk their lives to uncover the truth.

Relying solely on OSINT for intelligence gathering poses significant risks. Because OSINT is based on publicly available information, it is susceptible to manipulation. Adversaries can flood open-source channels with misinformation, misleading narratives, or irrelevant data to distract and confuse analysts. This tactic, known as "information laundering," can create a false sense of understanding and lead to incorrect assessments.

Moreover, OSINT is often used to confirm what has already happened rather than predict what will happen next. By the time information reaches the public domain, it is often too late to take preventative action. This reactive nature makes OSINT a poor choice for intelligence operatives that need to be several steps ahead of their adversaries to prevent attacks and protect national security.

In contrast, HUMINT allows for a proactive approach to intelligence. By cultivating sources within (or near-) terrorist organizations and building networks of informants, intelligence operatives can gain early warnings of potential threats. They can gather the kind of detailed, specific intelligence that is necessary to thwart plots before they come to fruition.

For instance, in the case of the Al-Qaeda plot uncovered by our HUMINT efforts, the intelligence gathered included the timing, targets, and methods of the planned attacks. This level of detail would never have been accessible through OSINT. It required operatives on the ground, working closely with sources who have direct knowledge of the plot and were willing to share it with us.

While HUMINT and OSINT are often viewed as competing forms of intelligence; the reality is that they are complementary. Each has its strengths and weaknesses, and the most effective intelligence operations leverage both to create a comprehensive picture. OSINT can provide valuable context and help identify potential areas of interest, while HUMINT can dig deeper to uncover the hidden truths that are critical to preventing attacks.

However, in high-stakes situations such as uncovering terrorist plots, HUMINT remains the cornerstone of effective intelligence work. It is the only method which can provide detailed, specific, and actionable intelligence needed to prevent attacks and protect innocent lives. OSINT can play a supporting role, but it is no substitute for the depth and reliability of HUMINT.

Sources and Credibility

In the world of intelligence, the integrity of the information hinges on the credibility of the sources who provide it. The discovery of any significant plot, such as the one detailed in this book, is fundamentally dependent on the quality, reliability, and authenticity of the sources involved. For the intelligence community, the process of assessing and verifying the credibility of sources is a meticulous and critical endeavor. In this chapter, we examine the complex nature of evaluating sources, understanding their backgrounds and motivations, and how these elements are crucial in distinguishing actionable intelligence from misinformation.

Source credibility in intelligence is about identifying who can provide information, and validating the fidelity of that information.Intelligence operatives operate under the constant threat of deception, misinformation, and manipulation, making the evaluation of source credibility an essential skill.

The first step in determining a source's credibility is a comprehensive assessment of their reliability. This involves a detailed examination of the source's background, affiliations, past behavior, and any previous interactions with intelligence agencies. The process of vetting a source includes a combination of psychological profiling, background checks, and often, polygraph examinations.

For instance, in the investigation of the Al-Qaeda plot, several sources were identified from within the terrorist organization. These individuals had extensive histories within the network. Evaluating their reliability involved understanding their positions within Al-Qaeda, their access to information, and their past credibility as informants. Intelligence operatives consider a source reliable if their information has proven accurate over time and if they have demonstrated a consistent alignment with the objectives of the operatives.

Understanding a source’s motivation is paramount in assessing the validity of the information they provide. Motivations can range widely, from financial incentives, ideological alignment, fear of reprisal, personal grievances, or even coercion.

Each motivation has a different impact on the reliability of the intelligence.

The Challenge of Vetting and Validating Information

Vetting a source and validating the information they provide is a continuous process that requires attention to detail and an understanding of the operational environment. Once a source has been assessed and deemed reliable, their information is subjected to rigorous validation processes, including cross-referencing with other intelligence disciplines such as signals intelligence (SIGINT), geospatial intelligence (GEOINT), and open-source intelligence (OSINT).

For example, details about the Al-Qaeda plot obtained through HUMINT were cross-checked with SIGINT, which included checking if the received screenshots and pictures were manipulated and if the IP addresses and telecom operators originated from the region. GEOINT confirmed locations of meetings and movements described by the sources. OSINT corroborated publicly available information and provided a broader context to the HUMINT details. This triangulation of data was essential to confirm the credibility of the intelligence and minimizing the risk of deception or misinformation.

The Attack on the United States and Europe

The Al-Qaeda plot, meticulously crafted over several years, represents the most sophisticated and ambitious terrorist operation conceived since the 9/11 attacks. This plot is a well-thought-out strategy deeply rooted in discussions which have taken place among Al-Qaeda's senior leadership over the last two decades. Figures such as Osama Bin Laden, Ayman al-Zawahiri, Saif al-Adl, and Hamza bin Laden have all contributed to its development, ensuring that it aligns with Al-Qaeda's evolving objectives and capabilities.

Historical Context and Strategic Evolution of the Plot

The roots of this plot can be traced back to the early 2000s when Osama Bin Laden and his closest advisors rethought their strategy in light of the growing U.S. military presence in the Middle East and the War on Terror. Bin Laden foresaw a prolonged conflict that would require innovative tactics and a global reach. While 9/11 was a shock to the system, the subsequent U.S. military response demonstrated to Al-Qaeda the need for a more decentralized approach.

The first outlines of this plan were found in an Al-Qaeda safehouse back in 2006. This was a plan to take a small part of Berlin. The current plot for 2024-2025 is multiplying that original plan in dozens of cities in the US and Europe with "Mumbai (India) -type" of attacks, or the ones in Beslan (Nort-Ossetia) or more recently in Moscow (Russia).

Over the years, Al-Qaeda adapted its strategy and learned from its successes and failures. After Bin Laden's death in 2011, Ayman al-Zawahiri and other leaders, like Saif al-Adl, continued to refine their approach, incorporating lessons learned from the conflicts in Iraq and Syria, the Arab Spring uprisings, and the rise and fall of ISIS. They recognized the fight against the West could not be won by direct confrontation alone but through a combination of guerrilla warfare, ideological indoctrination, and, most importantly, psychological operations aimed at breaking the enemy's determination.

This evolution in strategy became even more pronounced with the emergence of Hamza bin Laden as a key figure in Al-Qaeda. Hamza, often referred to as the "Crown Prince of Jihad," has been particularly vocal about expanding the battlefield to Western soil. He has repeatedly called for attacks that go beyond the symbolic and are designed to inflict real, lasting damage on Western societies. This plot is his vision brought to life: a sprawling, multi-pronged assault on the heart of the Western world.

The Impact of Geopolitical Developments

Recent geopolitical developments have provided Al-Qaeda with both the opportunity and the cover needed to execute such a complex operation. The fall of Kabul and the subsequent Taliban takeover of Afghanistan created a power vacuum which Al-Qaeda quickly exploited.

The Doha Agreement, brokered in February 2020 and meant to bring peace and stability, inadvertently facilitated Al-Qaeda's resurgence by legitimizing the Taliban and allowed them to consolidate control.

Furthermore, the chaos which followed the U.S. withdrawal devolved to a massive outflow of refugees and migrants, creating a unique opportunity for Al-Qaeda to embed its operatives within these populations. Senior leaders, including Saif al-Adl and Hamza bin Laden, anticipated this scenario years in advance. They understood amidst the waves of migrants, Al-Qaeda could move its fighters across borders, exploiting both legal and illegal routes to position themselves within the West.

The use of migration flows as a cover for moving operatives has been perfected over the years. The senior leadership of Al-Qaeda has long understood that in the age of mass migration and global displacement, blending in with refugees and asylum seekers provides an unparalleled opportunity to penetrate the enemy's defenses. This tactic has been refined and has become a cornerstone of Al-Qaeda's strategy in the West.

Abdul Azim Ali Musa bin Ali: The Key Player

Central to the operational success of this plot is Abdul Azim Ali Musa bin Ali, the Head of Al-Qaeda Covert Operations. Musa bin Ali's role is pivotal, because of his extensive experience in covert operations and his position in the Afghan Ministry of Interior (MOI). This dual role as a government official and a senior Al-Qaeda operative provides him with unparalleled access to official documents, including passports and travel permits, which he uses to facilitate the movement of Al-Qaeda operatives globally.

Musa bin Ali's history is a testament to his deep-rooted commitment to jihadist causes. Born in Libya, he was radicalized during his youth and quickly became involved in jihadist activities. He fought in Afghanistan in the 1990s, gaining invaluable experience in guerrilla warfare and covert operations. His subsequent travels took him to Iran, Iraq, Syria, and Turkey, where he honed his skills in intelligence gathering, logistics, and clandestine operations.

His return from Iran to Afghanistan in 2022 marked a new chapter in his career. Positioned within the MOI, he has been instrumental in issuing fake passports, creating false identities, and orchestrating the covert travel of Al-Qaeda operatives. His ability to manipulate official channels while remaining under the radar of Western intelligence agencies speaks to his skill and cunning. Musa bin Ali has effectively built a clandestine network which spans continents and connects dozens of terrorist groups, including all Al-Qaeda affiliates and almost all ISIS branches, ensuring Al-Qaeda operatives can move freely between Afghanistan, Pakistan, the Middle East, Africa, Europe and the US.

The Scale and Scope of the Plan

The sheer scale of this plot staggers Al-Qaeda plans to deploy at least 1,000 operatives to the United States and another 1,000 to Europe. These operatives are highly trained, battle-hardened fighters specifically chosen for their skills, experience, and commitment to the cause. They fought in almost all Jihadi combat-zones, Syria, Iraq, Libya, Somalia, Yemen and East- and West Africa.

Over the past few years, these fighters trained rigorously in Al-Qaeda's camps in Afghanistan and received orders for their part in this operation without telling them the full scale of the operation or details that could jeopardize the plan. They learned guerrilla warfare, urban combat, hostage-taking, bomb-making, and psychological warfare techniques.

Each operative is part of a small, highly autonomous cell, consisting of 8 to 12 members without up-front knowledge of that structure. These cells have been strategically distributed across major urban centers in the U.S. and Europe, with careful consideration given to cities with significant Muslim populations where they can blend in and potentially recruit local sympathizers. The selected cities in the U.S. are likely to include New York, Los Angeles, Chicago, Houston, and Washington, D.C., among others. In Europe, the focus will be on Western capitals such as London, Paris, Berlin, Madrid, Amsterdam, and Brussels, as well as other cities with sizable Muslim communities.

The Multifaceted Attack Strategy

The strategy for these attacks is multifaceted, combining elements of urban warfare, psychological operations, and insurgency tactics. Al-Qaeda's leadership has meticulously planned these operations to maximize impact and achieve strategic objectives.

For the execution of this plan a huge Operation Center is being developed in Afghanistan. All cells have their own 'team-leaders' who will provide instructions and who will be in constant contact with their cells. They will monitor local media to provide extra information to the cells as they did with the cells which conducted the Mumbai-attacks. This is an enormous operation which required years and years of planning, target selection and forming cells. Reliable sources also stated senior Al-Qaeda members, part of the group for at least twenty to thirty years, are being deployed to the countries to provide targets to the cells. Consequently, there will be local commanders with the different cells when the attack starts.

Coordinated Multi-Target Assaults

The initial phase of the attacks will involve a series of coordinated assaults on high-profile public venues. These include hotels, train stations, shopping malls, schools, religious centers, and popular cafes and restaurants. The goal is to create maximum chaos and confusion by attacking multiple locations simultaneously, overwhelming local law enforcement, and emergency responders.

The attackers will be heavily armed with automatic weapons, grenades, and improvised explosive devices (IEDs). They will employ tactics designed to maximize casualties and create a sense of panic among the civilian population. The use of fire, explosives, and chemical agents is not ruled out, as these methods can cause mass casualties and further hinder rescue efforts. Al-Qaeda's WMD project is in full operation.

Each cell will operate independently following a well-rehearsed plan and with flexibility to adapt to changing circumstances. This decentralized approach makes it difficult for authorities to predict their movements or coordinate a unified response. The simultaneous nature of the attacks is intended to stretch emergency services to their limits, reduce their ability to respond effectively, and increase the overall impact of the operation.

Targeting Security Forces, Critical Infrastructures and Economic Targets

In addition to civilian targets, some cells will focus on attacking local police stations, armories, and military facilities. The objective is to create confusion and divert resources away from the primary targets while capturing additional weapons and ammunition to sustain the operation.

These attacks on security forces, critical infrastructures and economic targets serve multiple purposes. They aim to demoralize law enforcement by demonstrating their vulnerability, disrupt communications and coordination efforts, and acquire the necessary resources to prolong the conflict. By attacking police stations and military outposts, the terrorists hope to create a perception of widespread anarchy and lawlessness, further undermining public confidence in the government's ability to maintain order.

Recruitment, Mobilization, and Expansion

A critical component of the plot is the effort to recruit and mobilize local Muslim populations to join the "Islamic army" in their respective regions. This call to arms will be broadcast through various channels, including social media, encrypted messaging apps, and traditional forms of communication like flyers and word of mouth.

The operatives will target communities with known sympathies towards extremist ideologies, including Salafist groups, local Islamist organizations, and disenfranchised youth. They will also seek to recruit returning ISIS fighters who have resettled in Europe but remain committed to the jihadist cause. By inciting a broader uprising and creating a local insurgency, Al-Qaeda hopes to expand the scale of the attacks and create a more prolonged and widespread conflict.

The recruitment strategy is not limited to ideological appeals; it also includes financial incentives and promises of status and power within the newly formed "Islamic army." By drawing on local support and leveraging existing networks of sympathizers and radicals, Al-Qaeda aims to transform the initial attacks into a full-scale insurgency, with the potential to destabilize entire regions.

Examination of this part of the plot provides us with a list of the potential targeted cities. The countries which participated in the Global war on terror Al-Qaeda sees as 'legitimate targets' with great potential for extra recruitment.

Areas within the United States, Spain, the Netherlands, Belgium, Germany, the United Kingdom, France, Sweden, Italy, Austria, and Canada have significant populations of migrants from the Middle East, Afghanistan and Pakistan and might be more inclined to support extremist causes:

United States

- New York City: Has a significant population from the Middle East and South Asia, particularly in neighborhoods like Jackson Heights, Queens, and parts of Brooklyn.
- Los Angeles: Home to a large Middle Eastern community, particularly in neighborhoods like Westwood ("Tehrangeles") with a large Iranian population.
- Detroit: Particularly the suburb of Dearborn, which has one of the largest Arab-American populations in the country, primarily Lebanese and Iraqi.
- Chicago: The city and its suburbs have substantial communities from the Middle East, particularly Palestinians, Jordanians, and Iraqis.
- Houston: Has a growing Pakistani and Middle Eastern community, especially in neighborhoods like Alief and areas near Hillcroft Avenue.
- The 'Twin-cities': The largest Somali community in the United States is found in the Twin Cities of Minneapolis and St. Paul, Minnesota. According to the most recent U.S. Census and American Community Survey (ACS) estimates, the Somali population in the U.S. ranges between 135,000 and 150,000. Of this, Minnesota, particularly the Twin Cities area, is home to an estimated 70,000 to 100,000 Somalis. This makes the Twin Cities the most significant hub for the Somali community in the country, with a well-established presence that includes Somali-owned businesses, mosques, and community organizations. We know Al-Shabaab, the Al-Qaeda affiliated group from Somalia, is involved in the upcoming attack.
- Clear potential targets: Washington, Las Vegas, Boston and Miami.

Spain

- Catalonia: Particularly in Barcelona, there is a significant Moroccan community. Catalonia has seen a notable number of radicalization cases in recent years, including the 2017 Barcelona attacks.
- Madrid: The capital also has a substantial Moroccan population. Some neighborhoods have been under surveillance due to concerns about radicalization.
- Ceuta and Melilla: These Spanish enclaves in North Africa have substantial populations of Moroccan descent and have seen some radicalization issues due to their unique geographic and socio-economic conditions.

The Netherlands

- Amsterdam: The capital has diverse immigrant communities, including significant populations from Turkey and Morocco. Some neighborhoods have been associated with higher risks of radicalization.
- The Hague: Known for having a considerable Muslim population, including people of Moroccan and Turkish descent. The Schilderswijk neighborhood has been particularly highlighted for radicalization concerns.
- Rotterdam: A port city with a large Moroccan and Turkish population. Some neighborhoods have higher rates of unemployment and social issues, contributing to radicalization concerns.

Belgium

- Brussels: Known for its large Moroccan community, particularly in neighborhoods like Molenbeek, which has been linked to several terror attacks and radicalized individuals.
- Antwerp: Home to a significant Muslim population, including Moroccans and Turks. Some areas in the city have seen issues related to extremism.
- Vilvoorde: A small town near Brussels that has had a disproportionate number of residents traveling to Syria and Iraq to join extremist groups.

Germany

- Berlin: The capital has a diverse immigrant population, including significant numbers from Turkey and Arab countries. Some neighborhoods have been flagged for radicalization risks.
- North Rhine-Westphalia: Cities like Duisburg, Dortmund, and Cologne have large Turkish and Middle Eastern communities. The state has seen some radicalization cases due to socio-economic factors.
- Hamburg: Has a substantial Turkish community and a history of Islamic radicalization cases, including links to the 9/11 attacks.
- Several other German cities might be involved in the upcoming attack.

United Kingdom

- London: The capital has a significant population of Middle Eastern, Pakistani, and Bangladeshi descent. Areas like East London (e.g., Tower Hamlets) have been noted for higher radicalization risks.
- Birmingham: Known for its large Pakistani community and has been associated with radicalization cases and extremist cells.

- Luton: A town with a notable Muslim population, including many of Pakistani descent, and has been highlighted in several terrorism-related investigations.

- Manchester: Particularly areas like Rusholme and Cheetham Hill have substantial Middle Eastern and South Asian communities. The city has seen notable terror-related incidents.

France

- Paris: and Suburbs: The capital and its surrounding suburbs (banlieues), particularly in Seine-Saint-Denis, have large populations of North African descent, including from Morocco, Algeria, and Tunisia. These areas have been linked to radicalization due to socio-economic challenges, high unemployment rates, and a sense of social exclusion among youth.

- Marseille: This port city in the south of France has a significant North African community. Some neighborhoods, like those in the northern districts, have been noted for radicalization concerns due to poverty, crime, and high unemployment.
- Lyon: Another city with a substantial North African and Middle Eastern community. Areas like Vénissieux and Villeurbanne have been highlighted for radicalization risks, partly duo to socio-economic challenges.
- Nice: Has a growing Muslim community, particularly of North African descent. The city has seen some terrorist attacks in recent years, increasing concerns about radicalization.

Sweden

- Stockholm: The capital has diverse immigrant neighborhoods, such as Rinkeby and Tensta, which have substantial populations from the Middle East, particularly Syria and Iraq. These areas have experienced issues related to integration and have been flagged for radicalization concerns.

- Gothenburg: Has a large Middle Eastern and North African community, particularly in the suburbs of Angered and Bergsjön. It has been noted for having one of the highest numbers of ISIS recruits per capita in Europe.
- Malmö: Known for its significant immigrant population, including from Iraq, Syria, and Afghanistan. Areas like Rosengård have been associated with radicalization due to socio-economic challenges and gang-related activities.

Italy

- Milan: The city and its suburbs have substantial populations from the Middle East and North Africa, including Egypt and Morocco. Some neighborhoods have been associated with radicalization due to economic difficulties and social exclusion.
- Rome: The capital has immigrant communities from various regions, including North Africa and the Middle East. While radicalization concerns are lower than in some other European capitals, certain areas still require monitoring.
- Bologna: Known for its North African population, including many from Tunisia and Morocco. The city has seen isolated cases of radicalization, especially among younger individuals.
- Naples: There is a growing population of migrants from the Middle East and North Africa in this southern city. The city has not seen significant radicalization but remains vigilant given its diverse population.

Austria

- Vienna: The capital has a substantial population from Turkey, the Middle East, and Afghanistan, particularly in districts like Favoriten and Ottakring. Some neighborhoods have seen radicalization cases, especially among second-generation immigrants.
- Graz: Austria's second-largest city has a growing Middle Eastern community and has been linked to some radicalization cases.
- Linz: While smaller than Vienna and Graz, Linz also has a notable immigrant population from the Middle East, especially in working-class neighborhoods.

Canada

- Toronto: The city and its surrounding suburbs (such as Scarborough and Mississauga) have large and diverse immigrant populations, including from Pakistan, Afghanistan, Iran, and other Middle Eastern countries. The Greater Toronto Area (GTA) has been noted for its diverse Muslim community, with some concerns about radicalization.
- Montreal: Has a substantial population from North Africa, particularly from Algeria and Morocco. The city has seen some cases of radicalization, particularly among youth in the suburbs of Saint-Laurent and Laval.
- Vancouver: Known for its diverse immigrant population, including a growing community from the Middle East and South Asia. While radicalization concerns are lower than in other cities, the city's diversity necessitates ongoing vigilance.
- Calgary: Has a notable Muslim community, including from Pakistan and the Middle East. The city has seen some instances of radicalization, particularly among youth influenced by global jihadist narratives.

Keep in mind that:

- Local radical Salafi and former jihadists will probably join in the first few days

- Just 10 Terrorists in Mumbai conducted 10 attacks, killing 170, in only 3 days

Notes:

- We do not know exactly what cities will be targeted. We do know it will be multiple cities in Europe and the United States, and the attacks will be simultaneous.
- We know the focus is on recruiting as many locals as possible, mainly the ones who fought in jihadi battlegrounds like Syria, Iraq and Somalia and who returned to the West following the collapse of the Islamic State.
- We know the Salafi communities in these cities with a large Muslim population are points of interest for Al-Qaeda because they understand the concept of Global Jihad and more likely to join the jihad.

Securing Territory and Establishing Control

The final phase of the plan involves securing and holding key areas within the targeted cities. By establishing control over strategic locations, such as major intersections, transportation hubs, public buildings, and residential neighborhoods, the terrorists aim to create semi-autonomous zones where they can operate with impunity.

These zones will be heavily fortified with makeshift barricades, booby traps, and IEDs. The terrorists are prepared to engage in prolonged firefights with police and military forces and will use hostages as human shields to deter any attempts to retake the territory. The goal is to hold these areas for as long as possible, creating a situation where the authorities are forced to negotiate or face continued bloodshed.

The establishment of these controlled zones serves multiple strategic purposes. It creates safe havens for the operatives, provides a base of operations for further attacks, and acts as a psychological blow to the government and security forces. By demonstrating their ability to seize and hold territory within major Western cities, the terrorists hope to inspire other jihadist groups and individuals to join their cause and replicate their actions in other parts of the world.

This recruitment of local jihadists will start in the wakes of the attacks to keep the uprising from the 'Islamic army' mission going.

Psychological Warfare and Propaganda

Central to the plot is the use of psychological warfare to amplify the impact of the attacks and achieve Al-Qaeda's broader objectives. The terrorists seek to create fear and uncertainty which extends far beyond the immediate areas of attack, affecting public perception and government policies globally

Manipulating the Media Narrative

Al-Qaeda has long understood the power of the media in shaping public perception and influencing political decisions. The plot includes a comprehensive media strategy designed to maximize coverage of the attacks and spread fear and panic across the globe.

The terrorists will use social media platforms and encrypted messaging apps to disseminate real-time updates and propaganda - showcasing their actions and calling for global jihad. They will also seek to exploit mainstream media coverage, knowing the more dramatic and violent the attacks, the more attention they will receive. By manipulating the media narrative, Al-Qaeda seeks to magnify the psychological impact of the attacks, creating a sense of vulnerability and helplessness among the general population.

The Significance of Symbolic Targets

The choice of targets is also deeply symbolic striking at the heart of Western culture and values.
By attacking iconic landmarks, bustling commercial centers, and symbols of affluence and power, the terrorists seek to send a clear message: nowhere is safe, and no one is beyond their reach.

This strategy is intended to create a sense of vulnerability and erode public confidence in the ability of their governments to protect them. By targeting places that people visit daily, such as cafes, hotels, and shopping malls, the terrorists aim to disrupt everyday life and create a lasting psychological impact. The fear generated by these attacks is intended to linger long after the physical damage has been repaired, affecting the social fabric and altering the way people live their lives.

Exploiting Social Media and Technology

In the digital age, social media and technology play a crucial role in shaping public opinion and influencing behavior. Al-Qaeda has adapted to this new reality, using social media platforms to recruit operatives, disseminate propaganda, and coordinate attacks. The terrorists will use social media to broadcast their actions live, providing a real-time narrative of the attacks and calling for others to join. They will exploit the viral nature of social media to spread fear and panic, knowing graphic images and videos of the attacks will be shared widely, amplifying their impact.

Al-Qaeda will also use encrypted messaging apps and other secure communication channels to coordinate their actions and maintain operational security. By leveraging technology, they will communicate with their operatives in real-time, adapt to changing circumstances, and ensure their message reaches a global audience.

A Global Call to Arms

The planned attacks are not merely acts of terror; they are intended to serve as a rallying cry for Muslims around the world to join the jihadist cause.

Hamza bin Laden's words encapsulate this vision: "What America and its allies fear the most is that we take the battlefield from Kabul, Baghdad, and Gaza to Washington, London, Paris, and Tel Aviv, and to take it to all the American, Jewish, and Western interests in the world."

By framing the attacks as part of a broader struggle against Western imperialism and oppression, Al-Qaeda hopes to inspire a new generation of jihadists to take up arms. The attacks are designed to be a catalyst for a global uprising, spark a wave of violence and unrest to destabilize Western societies.

Another important part, according to the Quran and Sunnah, is the obligations for the Islamic community to restore/re-conquer every inch of land that was once part of the Islamic world (the Caliphates).

Disenfranchised refugee youth in these cities will potentially join the attacks. There are small cells of young Afghans with a hatred towards the U.S. for abandoning their fathers in Afghanistan. Also, others could be co-opted through threats as their families still remain behind without any help from the West.

The Haqqani Network will play a vital role in the attack as Sirajuddin Haqqani deployed large numbers of Haqqani Network terrorists to the West. This is why he seeks to influence in many terrorist groups by letting them train in Afghanistan.

The bigger issue with the Haqqani's is their Network, and likely double agents, are providing information on groups like ISKP and AQIS to satisfy the West. The leaders of those groups are aware and even allow locational information to be shared on their senior leaderships based in Afghanistan, knowing Haqqani's will shield them from any operational efforts.

This way he is hiding where the primary threats are coming from and to distract from Al-Qaeda's plot against the U.S. homeland and European mainland.

This is a high-level game of chess, and the Haqqani's play a vital role in ensuring Al-Qaeda will achieve its goals.

The Potential Consequences

The potential consequences of this plot are dire. If successful, the coordinated attacks could result in thousands of casualties, widespread destruction, and a profound psychological impact on the targeted populations.

The attacks could also trigger a wave of copycat initiatives and inspire other jihadist groups and individuals to take action, leading to a broader, more sustained campaign of violence. This is why Sirajuddin Haqqani seeks to influence as many terrorist groups as possible at this moment.

As an example the Mumbai-attack contained 10 terrorists from one cell and conducted 10 terrorist attacks in 3 days killing 170 people. When multiplied by the +/- 200 cells which will participate in this simultaneous attack in the Western World, casualties could extrapolate to 34.000 deaths and 50.000+ injured.

March 11, 2004, Madrid, Spain, a series of bombings on commuter trains, executed by Islamist extremists linked to al-Qaeda caused 191 fatalities and injured over 2,000. November 13, 2015, Paris, France, coordinated attacks carried out by ISIS, resulted in 130 deaths and over 350 injuries. The assaults included suicide bombings and shootings at multiple locations including the Bataclan concert hall, various cafes, and restaurants. April 21, 2019, Sri Lanka, coordinated suicide bombings orchestrated by the National Thowheeth Jama'ath (NTJ), targeted churches and hotels in Colombo and other cities, which resulted in approximately 259 deaths and over 500 injuries.

The political ramifications will be severe. The attacks could lead to a rise in anti-immigrant sentiment, increased polarization, and a shift towards more authoritarian policies. Governments may be forced to enact stricter security measures, potentially infringing on civil liberties and leading to a backlash from the public. Al-Qaeda also hopes a part of the public actually blames the U.S. and believes they are complicit like 9/11. Al-Qaeda is banking the U.S. will blame ISIS as the U.S. continues to downplay al-Qaeda's threat.

This strategy is intended to create a sense of vulnerability and erode public confidence in the ability of governments to protect the general populace. By targeting places people visit daily, like cafes, hotels, and shopping malls, the terrorists seek to disrupt daily life and create a lasting psychological impact.

Preparing for the Worst

Considering these potential consequences, Western governments must prepare for the worst.

This includes enhancing intelligence gathering and sharing, improving border security, and increasing cooperation with allies and partners. It also requires a comprehensive counter terrorism strategy which addresses the root causes of radicalization and demotivates individuals from joining extremist groups.

Public awareness and preparedness are crucial. Governments must work to educate the public about the threat and ensure they know how to respond in the event of an attack. This includes promoting resilience and encouraging communities to stand together in the face of adversity.

Ultimately, the success or failure of this plot will depend on the ability of Western governments to anticipate and respond to the threat. While the scale and scope of the plot are unprecedented, it is not inevitable. With the right strategies and a coordinated effort, it is not possible to prevent the attacks, but countries can prepare counter-measures.

Projected Damage, Casualties and Effects

The potential impact of Al-Qaeda's plot to launch coordinated attacks across the United States and Europe is almost beyond comprehension. The scale, complexity, and sophistication of the planned operations indicate the damage and casualties could be catastrophic, surpassing all previous major terrorist attacks combined. This chapter examines the projected damage and casualties and the potential human, physical, and psychological toll these attacks could inflict on the targeted societies.

Projected Human Casualties

The primary and most devastating impact of these attacks would be the loss of human life. Drawing from historical precedents, we can estimate the potential casualties based on the tactics and targets outlined in the plot.

1. Simultaneous Attacks on Public Venues:

- The plot calls for coordinated assaults on hotels, train stations, shopping malls, schools, religious centers, and cafes across at least 10 major cities in the United States and dozens of European cities. If we consider past attacks like those in Mumbai (2008), where 10 terrorists killed 175 people, and extrapolate these numbers to the current plan involving hundreds of attackers, the potential casualties could be astronomical.

- Each cell, consisting of 8 to 12 operatives, is capable of killing dozens, if not hundreds, of people per attack. If 100 cells are active in the United States and another 100 in Europe, each carrying out attacks with the same efficiency and brutality as seen in Mumbai or the Paris attacks of 2015, the casualty figures could easily reach tens of thousands.

2. Targeting High-Density Areas:

- By focusing on high-density public spaces during peak hours, the attackers are likely to maximize casualties.

Train stations and shopping malls contain thousands of people depending on time of day. An attack involving automatic weapons, explosives, and possible incendiary devices in such an environment could lead to mass casualties within minutes.

- The terrorists' intention to take hostages further complicates the response, as it forces security forces into protracted standoffs where the risk of further loss of life is high. Past incidents, such as the Beslan school siege, show these situations often end in substantial casualties among hostages, attackers, and responding security forces.

3. Assaults on Critical Infrastructure and Security Forces:

- Attacks on police stations, military facilities, and other critical infrastructure are designed to divert law enforcement resources away from civilian targets, spreading chaos and confusion. These assaults are likely to result in significant casualties among security personnel and could incapacitate local law enforcement capabilities further exacerbating the situation.

- The attacks on security installations are designed to cause immediate casualties and capture additional weapons and ammunition to sustain further attacks potentially prolonging the violence and increasing the overall casualty count.

Potential for Secondary and Tertiary Casualties

There is a significant potential for secondary and tertiary casualties due to the nature of the attacks and the intended subsequent chaos.

1. Stampedes and Panic-Induced Injuries:

- The sudden onset of violence in crowded public spaces is likely to induce panic and chaos leading to stampedes and crush injuries. In previous terrorist attacks, such as those in Nice (2016) and Las Vegas (2017), many casualties occurred as people trampled each other.

- In densely populated urban environments, the risk of collateral injuries and deaths from such panic-induced stampedes is high potentially adding hundreds more to the casualty count.

2. Collateral Damage from Explosive Devices:

- The use of explosives, particularly in confined or enclosed spaces, can cause extensive collateral damage. Buildings can collapse, fires can break out, and secondary explosions can occur, all of which contribute to a higher number of casualties.

- In addition to the direct impact of explosive devices, the presence of hazardous materials in certain target areas (such as industrial sites or transport hubs) could result in secondary explosions or the release of toxic substances leading to further casualties and long-term health impacts.

3. Psychological Trauma and Long-Term Casualties:

- The psychological impact of such a large-scale, coordinated attack cannot be underestimated. Survivors and witnesses are likely to suffer from severe psychological trauma, including post-traumatic stress disorder (PTSD), anxiety, depression, and other mental health issues. Extra moral injury, especially by NATO veterans who fought and scarified in Afghanistan to prevent these types of attacks from occurring, might become a significant issue.

- The psychological toll of such an attack extends beyond the immediate victims. The fear and insecurity generated by these attacks can lead to a decline in public health. Stress and anxiety contribute to a range of physical and mental health issues. This long-term impact can result in a rise in suicide rates, domestic violence, substance abuse, and other indirect casualties

Projected Physical Damage

In addition to the human toll, the physical damage resulting from the attacks would be extensive, impacting infrastructure, property, and the broader urban environment.

1. Destruction of Public and Private Property:

- The use of explosives, automatic weapons, and incendiary devices would result in significant damage to public and private property.

Buildings would be damaged or destroyed, public transportation systems disrupted, and essential services incapacitated.

- The economic impact of such destruction would be profound, with businesses forced to close, infrastructure needing repair or replacement, and the potential for long-term disruption to the affected cities' economic and social life.

2. Damage to Critical Infrastructure:

- Attacks on critical infrastructure, including power grids, water supply systems, and communication networks, could have cascading effects, further exacerbating the immediate impact of the attacks. Disruption of these services would hinder emergency response efforts and contribute to the general chaos and panic potentially leading to additional casualties and damage.

- The targeting of transportation hubs, such as airports, train stations, and highways, would cripple the movement of people and goods, in the immediate aftermath and potentially for weeks or months as repairs are made and security measures are enhanced.

3. Long-Term Urban Impact:

- The long-term impact on urban environments could be severe. Areas targeted by terrorists would suffer from decreased property values, reduced investment, and an exodus of residents and businesses fearful of future attacks. This could lead to long-term economic decline and social decay in affected areas, further compounding the damage caused by the initial attacks.

Economic and Infrastructural Impact

The economic implications of the proposed attacks are equally dire, with far-reaching consequences which could ripple across global markets and lead to a significant economic downturn.

1. Immediate Economic Disruption:

- The immediate aftermath of the attacks would likely see stock markets plummet, consumer confidence erode, and a sharp increase in security costs. The closure of businesses, especially in the hospitality, retail, and transport sectors, would result in substantial economic losses.

- Insurance claims resulting from the damage and business interruption would be enormous, potentially overwhelming the capacity of insurance companies and leading to a financial crisis within the industry.

2. Long-Term Economic Consequences:

- The long-term economic impact would depend on the duration and scale of the attacks. If the terrorists manage to hold territory or sustain operations for an extended period, the economic consequences could be devastating, with entire regions potentially falling into recession.

- Increased security measures and heightened fear of further attacks could lead to decreased tourism, reduced foreign investment, and a general decline in economic activity. Governments would be forced to increase spending on defense and security, diverting resources from other critical areas such as healthcare, education, and infrastructure development.

3. Global Economic Repercussions:

- Given the interconnected nature of the global economy, the impact of these attacks would not be limited to the targeted countries. The shockwaves could spread to global markets, leading to a worldwide economic downturn.

- Supply chains would be disrupted, trade flows impacted, and global investor confidence shaken. The resulting economic instability could exacerbate existing tensions and conflicts, creating a feedback loop of violence and economic decline.

Societal and Political Implications

Beyond the immediate human and economic toll, the attacks are likely to have profound societal and political consequences, altering the fabric of the targeted societies and potentially reshaping global politics.

1. Social Fragmentation and Increased Polarization:

- The attacks are likely to exacerbate existing social tensions and contribute to increased polarization within the targeted societies. In the wake of such violence, fear and distrust of Muslim communities may rise, leading to a backlash against immigrants and refugees, further alienating these populations and potentially driving more individuals towards radicalization.

- The societal impact of such attacks would likely be felt for years, as communities struggle to rebuild trust and cohesion in the face of fear and suspicion. The rise of nationalist and xenophobic movements, already gaining momentum in many Western countries, could be further accelerated, leading to increased social fragmentation and conflict.

2. Erosion of Civil Liberties and Democratic Norms:

- In response to the attacks, governments may be forced to implement stringent security measures, potentially infringing on civil liberties and democratic norms. The balance between security and freedom is likely to shift towards the former, with increased surveillance, stricter immigration controls, and enhanced powers for law enforcement and intelligence agencies.

- This erosion of civil liberties could have long-term consequences, potentially undermining the democratic principles that underpin Western societies and creating a more authoritarian political climate.

- The erosion of civil liberties concern many people. Since the September 11, 2001 attacks, there have been notable instances where civil liberties and democratic norms in the U.S. have been perceived as eroded. The USA PATRIOT Act, enacted in 2001, expanded law enforcement powers for surveillance and data collection, raising concerns about privacy violations. The NSA's extensive surveillance programs, revealed in 2013, further fueled debates about government overreach and privacy infringements. The Guantanamo Bay detention facility, established in 2002, became controversial for holding detainees without trial and employing enhanced interrogation techniques, leading to criticisms of human rights abuses.

TSA security measures, such as full-body scanners and invasive pat-downs, sparked concerns about privacy. Lastly, no-fly lists and watchlists have faced scrutiny over due process issues and wrongful inclusions.

3. Geopolitical Ramifications:

- The attacks could have significant geopolitical ramifications, potentially leading to a realignment of global alliances and an increase in military interventions abroad. Western countries may be forced to adopt a more aggressive stance in the fight against terrorism, leading to increased military engagement in the Middle East and other regions.

- The attacks could also strain relations between Western countries and their allies, particularly those in the Muslim world. Efforts to counter terrorism may be seen as targeting Islam, leading to a backlash and further complicating international relations.

Psychological Warfare and Propaganda

Another important aspect is 'winning hearts & minds' in Western societies. They want to instill a fear of distrust in our governments. Also, they want a portion of the population to think it's justified, like a revolution, like we saw in the messaging with the Hamas attacks and the messaging in relation with the BLA attacks in Baluchistan, Pakistan.

Hamas utilizes psychological warfare and propaganda by framing its attacks as part of a righteous struggle against occupation and oppression. They present themselves as defenders of Palestinian rights, emphasizing their role in resisting a superior enemy and highlighting the suffering of Palestinians to garner local and international support. By executing high-casualty attacks, Hamas aims to instill fear and uncertainty within Israeli society, undermining public confidence in the government's ability to ensure safety. Additionally, Hamas seeks to draw global attention to their cause, hoping to increase international pressure on Israel and influence foreign governments and organizations to criticize or challenge Israeli policies.

The Balochistan Liberation Army (BLA) employs psychological warfare and propaganda by portraying its attacks as part of a broader struggle for Balochistan's independence and autonomy. They emphasize historical grievances and alleged injustices faced under Pakistani central government rule, seeking to build sympathy and support from human rights organizations and the international community. By targeting strategic infrastructure and military installations, the BLA aims to create instability and highlight the Pakistani government's inability to maintain order. Their propaganda also focuses on exposing alleged government abuses, aiming to mobilize local support by framing their actions as a fight against exploitation and neglect.

Another example: Al-Qaeda's leadership was surprised by the popularity of Bin Laden's 'Letter to America' under Western leftists, and the sympathies the younger generation showed to it. It made Al-Qaeda realize they can take advantage of their naivety.

Government Preparedness and Response

In light of the alarming threat posed by Al-Qaeda's planned large-scale attacks, government preparedness and response strategies must be comprehensive, proactive, and resilient. The complexity and scope of these potential attacks - targeting multiple major cities in the United States and Europe - demand an equally sophisticated approach to both prevent and respond to such incidents.

Understanding the Scope and Nature of the Threat

The foundation of any government preparedness plan is a thorough understanding of the threat. Current intelligence suggests that Al-Qaeda has trained and dispatched numerous operatives organized into small cells, all with the objective of executing simultaneous, multi-location attacks. This type of coordinated assault is designed to maximize casualties and instill widespread panic making it imperative for authorities to be fully aware of the potential risks.

To effectively counter such threats, governments must enhance their intelligence-gathering capabilities. This includes bolstering human intelligence (HUMINT) and signals intelligence (SIGINT) operations to detect and disrupt terrorist activities before they can be carried out. Close collaboration with international intelligence partners, particularly in regions where Al-Qaeda is known to operate, is essential. Advanced surveillance techniques, such as monitoring communications and financial transactions, must be employed to track the movements and activities of potential operatives

Additionally, inter-agency cooperation and international intelligence sharing are vital. The ability to connect disparate pieces of information across different agencies and borders can be crucial in predicting when the attack will occur. Governments should actively participate in international coalitions and task forces dedicated to counter-terrorism intelligence, ensuring a coordinated and unified response.

Conducting comprehensive risk assessments is another critical component of preparedness. Governments need to regularly evaluate the current intelligence landscape and analyze historical data on terrorist tactics and strategies. By understanding likely targets and attack methods, authorities can prioritize resources and focus preventive measures where they are most needed. Reviewing past incidents, such as the Mumbai and Paris attacks, can provide valuable insights and help identify potential vulnerabilities in security protocols.

Strengthening Domestic Security Measures

To effectively counter the diverse and widespread nature of Al-Qaeda's planned attacks, governments must enhance domestic security measures across multiple fronts, including physical security, emergency preparedness, and inter-agency coordination.

Key locations such as transportation hubs, public spaces, government buildings, and critical infrastructure should see increased patrols and surveillance. The deployment of advanced technology, including artificial intelligence-powered video surveillance and facial recognition systems, can significantly enhance monitoring and response capabilities. Additionally, quick reaction forces, such as SWAT teams and counter-terrorism units, should be on standby in major cities, ready to respond to any signs of an attack. These units need to be well-trained and equipped to handle high-stress scenarios involving hostages and heavily armed assailants.

Effective emergency response systems are crucial in minimizing casualties and restoring order in the aftermath of an attack. This requires enhancing communication channels between different emergency response agencies, such as police, fire services, medical personnel, and military units.

Establishing secure and redundant communication channels will ensure coordinated efforts during an attack, reducing response times and preventing confusion. Regular training exercises that simulate multi-location terrorist attacks can help prepare response teams for real-world scenarios, ensuring seamless coordination during an actual event.

Strengthening border and immigration controls is another essential aspect of government preparedness. Robust screening measures, including biometric data collection, background checks, and cross-referencing with international watchlists, are necessary to prevent the entry of potential terrorists even though most are probably already within our borders. Governments may also need to revise visa policies and travel regulations, particularly for countries with known terrorist activities to mitigate risks and enhance security.

Preparing for the Aftermath

Despite the best efforts to prevent an attack, this Al-Qaeda's plot will probably be executed as planned. Therefore, governments must prepare for the aftermath to minimize casualties, restore order, and prevent secondary attacks.

Developing crisis management plans is critical. Every major city should have a dedicated crisis command center capable of managing and coordinating a large-scale response. These centers should be equipped with state-of-the-art technology and staffed by experts from various fields, including law enforcement, emergency management, and public health. Clear and accurate communication with the public is also vital in the event of an attack to prevent panic and misinformation. Governments should have pre-established protocols for communicating with the public, utilizing social media, emergency broadcast systems, and other channels to provide timely updates and instructions.

Preparing medical and psychological support systems is equally important. Hospitals in major cities must be ready to handle mass casualty events, with plans in place for surge capacity, triage, and the rapid deployment of medical personnel. Stockpiling essential medical supplies and ensuring the availability of trauma care units and psychological support services are crucial components of preparedness. Additionally, governments should ensure that adequate mental health resources are available, including crisis counseling, support hotlines, and long-term care for survivors and first responders.

Establishing a legal and policy framework to support crisis management is another essential element of preparedness. Governments should review and, if necessary, enact emergency legislation that provides clear authority for actions such as curfews, evacuation orders, and the mobilization of military forces. This legal framework should be transparent and balanced, ensuring that civil liberties are respected while allowing for effective crisis management. Post attack recovery and reconstruction plans should also be developed in advance, detailing steps to restore infrastructure, provide support to affected communities, and ensure continuity of government operations.

Building Resilience and Community Preparedness

Government preparedness and response to terrorist threats extend beyond law enforcement and emergency services. Building resilience within communities and fostering public preparedness are also crucial components of an effective strategy.

Community engagement and awareness are vital in enhancing resilience. Public awareness campaigns that educate citizens about recognizing suspicious activities, responding to emergencies, and providing first aid can significantly improve community preparedness. Governments should offer training programs and resources to empower individuals and communities to take proactive steps in ensuring their safety. Encouraging community policing and local partnerships can help build trust between law enforcement and local communities, creating a network of support and vigilance that can be invaluable in preventing and responding to terrorist threats.

Strengthening cybersecurity and digital resilience is another important aspect of preparedness. As terrorist groups increasingly exploit digital platforms for communication, recruitment, and coordination, protecting critical digital infrastructure becomes paramount. Governments should invest in cybersecurity measures, including monitoring for cyber threats, securing sensitive data, and preventing digital sabotage. Promoting digital literacy and countering disinformation through public education can also help mitigate the impact of terrorist propaganda and misinformation.

International cooperation is essential in combating terrorism effectively. Governments should strengthen alliances and foster collaboration with international partners, sharing intelligence, best practices, and resources. Participating in global counter-terrorism initiatives and organizations, such as the United Nations, the Global Counterterrorism Forum, and regional security alliances, provides valuable opportunities for joint training, capacity building, and coordinated responses to emerging threats.

But... All of this is useless rhetoric since Governments, particularly the US Government, is 'sleeping' when it comes to the threats from the Taliban, Haqqani and Al-Qaeda. Due to politics, the current administration will not admi mistakes were made and by neglecting the threat we are facing, we are at a greater risk than ever before. The CIA and other Western Agencies produced statements Al-Qaeda has 'almost no capabilities' left in Afghanistan, while the facts show the opposite. Over 30 training camps, compared to the few they had before 9/11, say enough.

Overall Conclusion

In the wake of a renewed and restructured Al-Qaeda, the threat landscape for the United States and Europe has evolved into a far more dangerous and complex scenario than previously anticipated. Al-Qaeda's resurgence, particularly under the leadership of Hamza bin Laden and in collaboration with the Haqqani Network, signals a new phase in global jihadism. The group's ability to exploit geopolitical shifts, such as the fall of Afghanistan to the Taliban and the ensuing chaos has enabled it to rebuild and expand its operations to levels not seen since the pre-9/11 era.

The alarming reality of over 30 active training camps in Afghanistan, housing thousands of fighters from various jihadist factions worldwide, underscores the magnitude of the threat. These camps are havens for training; they are incubators for radicalization equipping operatives with the skills and mindset required for a global campaign of terror. The extensive network, which includes groups like Al-Qaeda in the Arabian Peninsula, Boko Haram, Al-Shabaab, and even elements of ISIS, reveals a united front against the West which is more dangerous and ideologically cohesive than ever.

The revelation of the plot to launch widespread, coordinated attacks in Western cities marks a significant escalation in Al-Qaeda's strategy. These planned assaults, reminiscent of the Mumbai-style attacks but on a far grander scale, aim to create chaos, instill fear, and cause maximum casualties. The plot, meticulously designed over several years by top Al-Qaeda leaders and covert operatives, reflects a sophisticated understanding of Western vulnerabilities and a ruthless intent to exploit them.

Moreover, the collaboration between Al-Qaeda and state actors such as Iran highlights a troubling nexus of interests. Iran's strategic decision to provide sanctuary and support to Al-Qaeda members has facilitated the group's operations, allowing for easier movement, coordination, and execution of plans across multiple continents. This partnership underscores the complexity of the threat, as it involves not just non-state actors but state-sponsored entities with their geopolitical agendas.

Despite these challenges, it is imperative that governments, intelligence agencies, and law enforcement authorities do not succumb to despair. The discovery of this plot, while alarming, also presents an opportunity for a robust and decisive response. It is a stark reminder of the importance of HUMINT and the critical role that human intelligence plays in uncovering and thwarting such threats.

Governments must not only enhance their security measures but also foster greater inter-agency and international cooperation. The fight against terrorism is not confined to borders; it is a global battle that requires a unified, coordinated response. Sharing intelligence, resources, and expertise is not just beneficial - it is essential for success.

In addition to bolstering defenses and intelligence efforts, there is a critical need to address the underlying factors that fuel radicalization and recruitment. This involves not only military and law enforcement strategies but also socio-political and economic interventions that can undermine the narratives used by groups like Al-Qaeda to justify their actions and attract followers.

The projected impact of these planned attacks will be catastrophic. The loss of life, psychological trauma, societal disruption, and economic consequences will be unprecedented. The psychological and societal effects will ripple through communities, creating divisions and potentially fueling further radicalization. Economically, the ramifications will trigger a global recession, exacerbating inequalities and creating fertile ground for extremism.

To mitigate these potential outcomes, governments must invest in comprehensive preparedness and response strategies. This includes strengthening critical infrastructure, enhancing cybersecurity, improving emergency response capabilities, and fostering community resilience. Public safety measures and awareness campaigns can empower citizens to act as the first line of defense, recognizing and reporting suspicious activities and supporting community-based prevention efforts.

Ultimately, the fight against terrorism is a collective endeavor which requires the commitment of governments, organizations, and individuals. It demands vigilance, resilience, and a steadfast commitment to the values of democracy, freedom, and justice.

As we move forward, it is crucial to recognize the war against terrorism cannot be won on the battlefield. It is a struggle for the hearts and minds of people across the globe. By addressing the root causes of extremism, promoting dialogue and understanding, and ensuring justice prevails over revenge, we can hope to build a world where the ideologies of hate are defeated by the enduring values of peace, respect, and human dignity.

The path ahead is fraught with challenges, but it is not insurmountable. With resolve, unity, and a clear-eyed understanding of the threat, we can confront and ultimately overcome this new wave of terrorism.

The stakes could not be higher, but neither could the determination of those who stand in defense of our shared future.

Acknowledgments

Writing this book has been an incredibly rewarding journey, made possible by the invaluable collaboration, support, and insights from numerous individuals. Without their contributions, this work would not have reached its full potential.

First and foremost, we extend our deepest gratitude to Guido Blaauw. His unparalleled expertise, relentless dedication, and deep understanding of global jihad, Islam, Al-Qaeda, and Afghanistan were the backbone of this project. His commitment to seeking the truth and his vision in shaping the direction of this book have inspired us all. Guido, your contributions were nothing short of extraordinary, and this work bears the mark of your profound influence.

To Sarah 'SUPERBAD' Adams, your meticulous attention to detail and your thorough fact-checking were instrumental in ensuring the highest standards of accuracy and reliability throughout the book. Your tireless efforts and commitment to excellence have significantly enriched the quality of this work. Thank you for bringing your vast expertise and sharp focus to every aspect of this project.

A heartfelt thank you goes to Ivett Zsuró-Luz, whose incisive analytical skills and critical feedback helped refine the key ideas and arguments within these pages. Your groundbreaking research and your invaluable background knowledge helped shape this book into something much greater. Ivett, your contributions are a beacon for those pursuing knowledge and truth in a complex world.

We owe special thanks to Russ "GRANDPA" Pritchard, who's extensive on-the-ground insights provided invaluable context to this book. Your dedication to truth, the intelligence community, and relentless efforts to save our Afghan Allies shine a light on the realities of this world and have left an indelible mark on this book. Thank you for your tireless support, expertise, and NEVER QUIT / ALWAYS HERE mantras.

Lastly, we owe an immeasurable debt of gratitude to our brave HUMINT sources in Afghanistan. Your unwavering commitment to uncovering the truth in the face of unimaginable danger is nothing short of heroic.

You risk your lives daily, not just for the sake of intelligence, but to give a voice to the silenced, and to protect the future of your homeland. Your courage, resilience, and dedication represent the very best of your nation. In the darkest moments, you have been the light that guides us toward understanding, and for that, we are eternally grateful. Your sacrifices will never be forgotten, and your efforts stand as a testament to the strength and dignity of your people. You are Afghanistan's true heroes, its unwavering defenders.

This book is a testament to your hard work, dedication, and commitment to making the world a safer place.

Thank you all.

Appendix 1.

List of major Al-Qaeda (or Al-Qaeda affiliated-) Attacks[1]

Year:	Location:	Attack:	Killed:
1992	Yemen	Aden Hotel bombings	2
1993	USA	1st World-trade bombing	6
1995	Saudi Arabia	Attack US facility in Riyadh	7
1998	Kenya, Tanzania	US Embassy bombings	224
1998	France	World Cup terror plot (failed)	0
2000	Yemen	USS Cole bombing	17
2000	France	Failed Strasbourg Cathedral bombing plot	0
2001	Afghanistan	The assassination of Ahmad Shah Massoud	1
2001	Europe	Plan to attack several US targets in Europe	0
2001	USA	The 9/11 Attacks	2.996
2001	USA	Failed ‘shoe-bomber’ Richard Reid	0
2002	Tunesia	The Ghriba Synagogue bombing	19
2002	Yemen	The Limburg ship bombing	1
2002	Kuwait	Attack on US marines Faylaka Island	1
2002	Indonesia	Bali bombings	202
2002	Kenya	Mombasa Attacks against hotel and plane	13
2002	Morocco	Failed plot to attack warships in Gibraltar	0
2002	United Kingdom	Failed ‘Wood Green ricin plot’	0
2003	Saudi Arabia	Riyadh compound bombings on expats	39
2003	Morocco	The Casablanca bombings	45
2003	Indonesia	The Jakarta Marriott Hotel bombing	12
2003	Turkey	Istanbul bombing synagogues & UK Emb.	57
2004	Spain	Madrid train bombings	193
2004	Saudi Arabia	The Khobar attacks	22
2007	United Kingdom	London attacks on bus and subway	56
2005	Jordan	The Amman bombing Palestinian wedding	57
2006	Germany	Failed German train bombings	0
2006	UK/USA	Failed transatlantic aircraft plot	0
2007	Algeria	AQIM attack at the government Palace	33
2007	Pakistan	Failed assassination of former PM Bhutto	0
2007	Algeria	AQIM attack at Algerian court and UN staff	41
2007	Germany	Failed bomb plot from the Sauerland Cell	0
2007	Denmark	Failed Copenhagen bomb plot	0
2007	United Kingdom	Failed plot to behead a British soldier	0
2008	Pakistan	Attack on the Danish Embassy	6
2008	Afghanistan	Battle of Wanat (500 Talib vs. 72 US/ANA)	9
2008	India	Mumbai bombings Lashkar-e-Taiba	166
2008	Spain	The failed Barcelona Terror plot	0
2009	Yemen	Failed AQAP attack North-West flight 253	0
2009	Afghanistan	Camp Chapman attack on a CIA compound	8
2009	USA	Failed bomb plot NY Subway	0
2010	India	Attack on a German Bakery	17

[1] Not included: the thousands of attacks to gain territorial power in the larger jihadi-conflict area's like; Afghanistan, Pakistan, Syria, Iraq, the Sahel, Yemen and Somalia.

Year:	Location:	Attack:	Killed:
2010	Yemen	The failed AQAP Cargo Planes bomb plot	0
2010	Algeria	The Amenas hostages, killing foreigners	39
2010	Denmark	Failed Copenhagen ('Mumbai style') plot	0
2010	Denmark	Failed bomb-letter, explosion at Hotel	0
2012	Libya,	Benghazi Attacks at US embassy and CIA	8
2014	Norway	Foiled Ansar-al-Islam Norway terror threat	0
2015	France	AQAP attack on Charlie Hebdo in Paris	12
2016	Somalia	Failed Daallo Airlines flight 159 bombing	0
2017	Russia	Saint Petersburg Metro bombing	15
2019	United Kingdom	London bridge stabbing	3
2020	United Kingdom	Reading stabings	3
2020	Germany	Dresden knife attack	1
2021	Afghanistan	Taliban and Al-Qaeda taking over the country on August 15th	
2021	Afghanistan	Haqqani & ISK HKIA Airport bombing	183
2024	Somalia	Hotel attack Mogadishu	32

Made in the USA
Columbia, SC
02 January 2025

51066887R00062